Spread *This* Wealth
(And Pass *This* Ammunition!)

Why We *Must*, and How We *Can* Save America
From Its Own Misguided Government

C. Jesse Duke

Spread *This* Wealth (and Pass *This* Ammunition!): Why We Must, and How We Can Save America From Its Own Misguided Government

Copyright © 2009 by C. Jesse Duke. No part of this book may be used or reproduced without written permission of the publisher, except for excerpts that may be used in brief quotations, giving proper credit, and in critical reviews.

ISBN-13   978-0-9815559-3-5
Bible quotations are from the New King James Version
Dictionary quotes are from Merriam-Webster's New Collegiate Dictionary, Eleventh Edition

Printed in the United States of America

Encouraging Word Press, Inc.
www.encouragingwordpress.com

Cover design by e-moxie.com

I dedicate this book to the people who wrote and signed this:

We hold these truths to be self-evident, that all men are created equal, that they are endowed by their Creator with certain unalienable Rights, that among these are Life, Liberty and the pursuit of Happiness. — That to secure these rights, Governments are instituted among Men, deriving their just powers from the consent of the governed, — That whenever any Form of Government becomes destructive of these ends, it is the Right of the People to alter or to abolish it, and to institute new Government, laying its foundation on such principles and organizing its powers in such form, as to them shall seem most likely to effect their Safety and Happiness. Prudence, indeed, will dictate that Governments long established should not be changed for light and transient causes; and accordingly all experience hath shewn that mankind are more disposed to suffer, while evils are sufferable, than to right themselves by abolishing the forms to which they are accustomed...

— American Declaration of Independence, 1776

Acknowledgments

I want to thank my family for their help as I worked many hours beyond my day job to research and write this book. Thank you, to all of my fellow citizens, who show up at tea parties with great signs and even greater enthusiasm for the cause of liberty. I especially like the signs that say, *"I'll keep my guns, my money, and my freedom. You can keep the change!"* and *"If I cheat on my taxes can I get a cabinet position?"* I also acknowledge the people who have been fighting for the Fair Tax for ten years now. Thank you for all your research and analysis, as well as your communication of these timely ideas. I believe, and feel in my bones, that the time has come for the Fair Tax. So hang in there and see the fruits of your labor blossom. I especially thank all the current and past members of the military. If it weren't for patriots like you, guys like me couldn't write books like this!

"I think when you spread the wealth around, it's good for everybody."

— Barack Obama

"When the people find that they can vote themselves money, that will herald the end of the republic."

— Benjamin Franklin

Contents

Acknowledgments 5
Introduction 9

Chapter One
Was It Just a Dream? 23

Chapter Two
American Values and Founding Principles 35

Chapter Three
Says Who? 47

Chapter Four
Pretty Rocks 59

Chapter Five
What's Wrong With Socialism? 72

Chapter Six
Parallel Nations 90

Chapter Seven
The Five-Step Plan to Save America 99

Chapter Eight

The Fair Tax 110

Chapter Nine

Get Back to the Constitution 130

Chapter Ten

Right Revolution 141

Appendix A 153
Appendix B 158
Appendix C 161
Endnotes... 162
About the Author................................ 165
About the Cover................................. 166

Introduction

One cold, December day in 1777, a farmer was walking along a creek near Valley Forge when he heard a voice coming from within the woods. The farmer crept toward the sound but saw only a lone white horse tied to a tree. Investigating further, he found the owner of the voice. It was General George Washington, on his knees in the snow, praying. Back at the General's camp, men were sick and starving, with feet bleeding for lack of shoes, and morale was ebbing quickly.

The farmer quietly slipped away. When he got back home, he told his wife, *"The Americans will win their independence! George Washington will succeed!"*

Doubtfully, his wife asked, *"What makes you think so?"*

"I saw him in the woods today, and I heard him praying! If there is anyone on this earth that the Lord will listen to, surely it is this man."

The citizens of the United States of America are the most fortunate people who have ever walked the face of the earth. Through the sheer grace of God, the courage of the men and women who fought for our freedoms, and the genius of our Founders, we have been able to enjoy a level of freedom and prosperity never before seen in the world.

In order to prosper financially, humans must be free to pursue their dreams. The individual pursuing goals that he or she is passionate about is what makes for dynamic and robust economies. Repression of individual freedom, either through coercive government or oppressive taxation is the drag on the human spirit that simply need not be. Wise and humble leaders make way for freedom because freedom is the condition necessary for prosperity. Freedom has enabled Americans to grow rich in millions of ways, each individual pursuing his or her own God-given dreams. It is American freedom that has given the world an abundance of life-saving and life-enhancing innovations. Advances in technology, medicine, science, and transportation—just to name a few—have made the lives of countless millions of people around the world better, and even possible.

Our government was charged from the beginning with the duties to protect and defend our freedoms.[1] How fortunate we have been to have had many humble leaders who have understood the origins of our basic human rights and who restrained themselves from the lure of personal power out of a sense of responsibility to God and to future generations! At the same time, a majority of citizens have understood and adhered to a unique American culture that respects individual liberty and personal responsibility. **America could never have progressed as fast and as far as it has without this wedding of liberty and responsibility.** It was the wisdom to wed, and then maintain, these principles of personal responsibility and individual liberty that made America great. By passing along this standard to each succeeding generation, America has been able to maintain its strength.

But we began divorce proceedings in the early Twentieth Century. Some would say that it began with the social programs of the New Deal in the 1930's. But without the establishment of the income tax in 1913, the New Deal would never have happened. Now, it is quite evident that many, inside government and in the wider culture, have lost the appreciation for liberty and the wisdom required to maintain it.

As a society we have delegated to government what no government can do. We have given over the responsibility for our individual lives to government and the proof is in the bills that are passed by Congress without having even been read; in the entitlement checks printed by the Treasury with no money to back them except what will be earned by our children and grandchildren; and in the condescending speech of government officials at all levels.

When individuals give the responsibility for their well-being to government, they also give up their liberty. When individuals are no longer self-sufficient, they look to government for every need and want they have. Recently a woman in California was upset when a fast-food restaurant did not give her the correct order. What was her course of action? She called government! She got on her cell phone and dialed 911 so that someone in authority could solve her problem for her. We hear stories like this and we think about how stupid some people can be and we laugh. But, in essence, millions of our fellow citizens solve their life-problems this way. They call on government for everything, and they seek politicians who will promise them that they will solve all of their problems if elected or re-elected.

The term we use for this paternalistic government is socialism. To escape the negative connotation of socialism, some have started calling it "progressivism." **No matter what it's called, it is a worldview that has led us into the biggest self-inflicted economic and moral train wreck in history.** We are now a debtor nation. We're broke, in more than our finances.

Much has been said about socialism ever since candidate Obama told Joe the Plumber that he wanted to "spread the wealth" by taxing the "rich" to give to the poor and middle class. His statement seemed to embolden others with similar ideas, to step up their efforts to socialize America. I was one of many who was shocked to see just how widespread this bad idea had become among my fellow citizens. Huge flocks of followers applauded the ideas presented by the new President. And, sad to say, those who tried to explain what was wrong with this "progressive" approach to governance were quickly drowned out by the bleating masses, and were simply ignored, or even ridiculed, by a sycophantic press.

Laying aside the fact that socialism has always had extremely detrimental results wherever it has been tried, I decided to give the concept some serious reflection in the light of my own life experience and education. I have come to see that the President was right. We *do* need to "spread the wealth," the true wealth, that has made America the beacon of liberty and hope for millions around the world. Only by spreading this immense wealth of our founding principles and values can we save America from the overwhelming debt, oppressive taxation, and tyrannical public policies that threaten our very existence as a free nation.

The true wealth of America is not in our bank accounts, but has been paying dividends to the descendents of our Founders for 233 years. This vast storehouse of wisdom was behind our rise to becoming the beacon of freedom to millions. Even those who do not adhere to our founding principles are blessed by their overflow. Even our enemies are beneficiaries of the by-products of our freedom.

I list and explain these founding values and principles in Chapter Two. But first, I hope to awaken the desire in my fellow citizens for the blessings of liberty and liberty's Creator, and to pass the ammunition of education to you so you, in turn, will pass it along to others. This ammunition consists of many good resources containing rich treasures of American principles and values. I list them in the "Ammunition" section, Appendix A, in the back of the book.

The phrase, *"Pass this ammunition,"* comes from a saying used by soldiers and sailors during World War II. The entire saying was, *"Praise the Lord, and pass the ammunition."* I first heard it from my father who served on the *USS Essex* aircraft carrier in the Pacific. As with most slang terms, the origin of this one is not clear; but it was made into a song during the war. Patriots used it to encourage each other. Their perspective was that, although they had to do the dangerous and dirty work of fighting a tough enemy, their cause was just and necessary, and they believed God was strengthening them. **We would do well to remember the truth of these words, because we are now facing an enemy more insidious than any in uniform. Our enemy is the silent, creeping menace of our very own government, which we ourselves are feeding.** No foreign power could ever inflict as much damage to us as our own government is doing. Our ammunition is, of course, not bullets or bombs, but ideas, principles, and values — the weapons that the Founders passed along to us in hopes that we would use them to keep this republic going.

Somewhere along the way, we got the idea that people who manage to get themselves elected to Congress and the Presidency, and appointed to the Supreme Court, have more brains than the rest of us. And we've surrendered much of our futures, in the form of exorbitant and immoral taxation, to a machine that has grown so big and cumbersome that it knows not what it does, nor does it seem to care.

One recent example of this was discovered in early May 2009. The Medicare system had paid out over sixty billion dollars in fraudulent claims by bogus companies! To make matters worse, the President announced within three days of that discovery that he was proposing to raise our taxes by sixty billion dollars over the next ten years! I suppose this was an unfortunate coincidence, but it clearly illustrates the problem with big government. This was just a whitecap upon the tsunami of government waste and fraud. The right hand of government does not know what the left hand is doing, and both hands are throwing money around like it's only paper. It's not just paper. It is our very lives being squandered in a thousand reckless, manipulative ways.

For far too long, we have accepted the idea that government knows best. The results have been disastrous. Our national debt is now at eleven trillion dollars! That debt has come about just as it does in any family. We have lived beyond our means for too long, overspending, and wasting money on things we really don't need. Instead of enhancing our security, we spent to enhance the national *lifestyle*. Now the time of reckoning has arrived.

To grasp just how much a trillion dollars is, look at it this way: A million dollars is a thousand thousands. A billion dollars is a thousand million. A trillion dollars is a thousand billion. If you were to try to pay back the current national debt at a rate of a million dollars a day, it would take approximately thirty-two thousand (32,000) years to pay off eleven trillion dollars! And that's not even figuring in the eight-hundred fifty billion dollars in interest you'll be paying every year! (I hope you're taking good care of yourself.)

Of course, you'll never pay it off, and neither will your children or their children. But they will be taxed to the hilt to pay for the extremely poor decisions and bad behavior of our generation. Later in this book, I'll show you how this taxation equals modern-day slavery.[2] I'll also show you a solution that is available to us right now, if we have the courage to implement it.

During World War II, German pastor and theologian, Dietrich Bonhoeffer, stood up to Nazi aggression. He said, *"The ultimate test of a moral society is the kind of world it leaves to its children."* He was later hanged in a Nazi concentration camp. How can we as mature adults lay this unimaginable burden of debt and its attending bondage on future generations? The fact that we have borrowed trillions of dollars from our children and grandchildren to finance lifestyles, including government lifestyles, shows that a clear moral boundary has been crossed.

We all know, or should know, that when a family finds itself in debt, the adults have to make some tough decisions. They first must quit borrowing, then *drastically* cut spending—except for the essentials such as food, shelter, and debt payments. Then they have to find ways to increase income so they can pay off the debt. Once the debt is paid off, the last step is to establish an emergency fund so the family does not end up going into debt again when the inevitable crisis comes. These are the same simple steps we need to force our representatives to take on a national level. But in order to take those four steps, we need to take the preliminary step of replacing all the representatives in Congress who have already proven they are not up to the task with patriots who understand and appreciate the original intent of the Founders.

Just as a family is subject to the laws of finance, so also is our government. No one in his right mind would go out and borrow more money when he is already in the hole. Yet this is what our government has done for seventy years, and now it has gone beyond the limits of outrageousness! It's as if the children are running the family budget. It's time for the adults, the average citizens of this country, to take charge.

I am aware that government has never been without debt. But just because "we've never done it that way" before doesn't mean it can't be done. Nor does it mean we should not have freedom from debt as a goal. Having debt-freedom as a goal will keep us from borrowing more and focus us on *at least* paying down the debt. That is far superior to having no goal, which guarantees more and more borrowing.

In Chapter Seven you will find the simple Five-Step plan for saving America from government: **Stop borrowing, cut spending, pay off the debt, increase income by replacing the income tax**

with the Fair Tax, and establish an emergency fund. The Fair Tax is in bill form at both the Senate and the House of Representatives right now, and has been for ten years! The benefits of such a radical change in the way taxes are collected in this country are numerous. The first benefit is the repeal of the Sixteenth Amendment, which established the income tax, the most counterproductive drag on economic growth and prosperity ever devised!

The reason the Fair Tax has not been enacted yet is that it takes power to manipulate our lives away from Congress. **The enactment of the Fair Tax would be the single most powerful thing we can do to ensure freedom and prosperity for future generations.** In fact, if we do not elect people who support the Fair Tax wholeheartedly, none of the other steps — stop borrowing, cut spending, increase income, pay off the debt, and establish an emergency fund — can be successful. I discuss the Fair Tax under the step to increase income because that is the only way we can increase revenue to government without raising taxes. Once Congress has begun the the Five-Step plan, they can begin to implement the other items on the "Get Back!" flag.

America is not its government, or even the people in the government. America is a spirit. It is the freedom that has always lived in every human heart. America was not "founded" as much as it was discovered. It was predestined for its place in human history. Like a mirage that turned out to be real, it became an oasis for all people who thirst for freedom. If we let that watering hole dry up, we will be condemning ourselves and future generations to another long, bloody struggle for freedom. We, who are living in America now, have the moral imperative to restore Constitutional limits and fiscal responsibility on the United States government to preserve America for future generations.

Too many of our fellow citizens have lost sight of what made this country great. The United States was not made great by government, but by good, hard-working people who stood up for the principles of liberty and against the onslaughts of tyranny. Many Americans have drifted so far from these principles that they can't even hear the printing presses at the Treasury hammering out the shackles for their children and grandchildren.

But there is good news! The spirit that inspired and motivated the patriots at Valley Forge to endure is alive and well today, as seen in the tenacity and heroism of the young men and women who have persevered in Iraq over the last six years. They not only had to overcome the cowardly insurgents who daily killed their fellow soldiers and innocent civilians with hidden bombs, but they also had to persevere against the cowardly politicians and left-leaning news media that daily sided with the enemy! They prevailed against enormous odds! My hope is that those who read or hear this book will understand how precious, and yet how fragile, American freedom is today, and that they will take the example of our military and stand for freedom against the insurgency of the socialists in the United States.

Lest anyone think I'm some sort of anti-government extremist, let me assure you that I love this country and its Constitution. That's why I'm trying to save it from the well-meaning, but ill-informed people who have managed to get themselves into positions of power. Those politicians who vote to recklessly spend in spite of the debt, who vote to interfere in the free market by bailing out poorly run companies and irresponsible individuals, and who continue to work for more social welfare spending and punitive taxation, are the ones we must get rid of in the elections of 2010 and 2012. The majority of such people in Congress today do not even see the economic tsunami coming and have no incentive to change. This is evidenced by the fact that they are still spending! At the time of this book's publication, they are getting ready to vote on a trillion dollar socialized health care plan, even though a large majority of Americans say they are satisfied with their health care plans![3] Instead of just dragging the few who want government health care into the dependency net, then leaving the rest of us alone, Congress is on course to nationalize all of us, making millions of Americans' health care more expensive, less efficient, and more deadly!

The solutions to all of our economic, political, and spiritual problems lie in education. Unfortunately, we cannot rely on the currently established education system. It has helped to perpetuate the historic and economic ignorance that has caused our current dilemma. We, as citizens, must renew the spirit of self-reliance, individual responsibility, and freedom in America. It is imperative that we do so. In the chapters that follow, I give a simple explanation of the *foundations* of freedom and why you, the reader, the individual, have an immensely important role to play in the history of America, and indeed, all mankind.

Before I go on, I'll tell you who I am. I'm just a simple, ordinary citizen. I'm not rich, smart, or good looking. I make my living with my hands, as I have for almost forty years. I have the same qualifications for writing this book that you have: the First Amendment to the Constitution and an access to history and economics resources. You have access to all the same information I have. I'm just condensing it into book form for those of you who are too busy making a living, paying your taxes, and raising your families to gather all the economic and spiritual information necessary to fight the good fight.

I also have another, more compelling reason to write this book. I first took the United States Oath of Office when I joined the Marines in 1973. I raised my right hand and swore to "...*defend the Constitution of the United States against all enemies, foreign and domestic...*"[4] Unlike many past and present members of Congress, I took that oath seriously, without reservation or purpose of evasion. I believe the Constitution has been ignored, assaulted, and maligned for many years now, but that the current onslaught of spending, borrowing, czaring, and passing of unread bills has broken the proverbial camel's back. I believe there are millions of current and former military and other government servants who have taken the same oath to defend the Constitution who are horrified at the outrageous encroachments on liberty going on today. Let me say to you now, that your swearing of that oath was not a passing, nor a light matter. **It was, my friends, for such a time as this.**

We all stand on the shoulders of great men and women who have defended freedom for the 233-year existence of our nation. But before the United States of America was established, colonies of men and women stood up against political tyranny in other places and times. Throughout history, hundreds of thousands have died, many more have been maimed for life, and their countless families have endured unspeakable hardships to bring about the freedoms we have so undeservingly inherited. I'm not worthy to be counted among those heroes and martyrs. I'm just a grateful beneficiary of their sacrifices, and I take pride in the fact that this nation was settled, built, and defended by ordinary people, just like me—laborers, lumberjacks, farmers, soldiers, share-croppers, and others who make their living by the sweat of their brow. I take pride in the fact that I'm one of them and not an intellectual. All I have to offer are some common sense solutions. I'm sure the elites will just ignore me, but I think there are millions of people who will read, agree, and act.

Up until April 15th, 2009, I felt like the Chinese guy standing in front of the tank in Tiananmen Square. Then I went to a tea party. In case you haven't heard of the recent tea parties, they are impromptu, informal gatherings of citizens who are fed up with the income tax, the national debt, agenda-driven news media, and subjugation of Americans by excessive legislation. Now I know I'm not alone in this battle. If you are an average citizen like me, and you're feeling powerless, don't. Here is a plan to get your power back. Government should work for us, not us for government. You know it. I know it. And millions of our fellow citizens know it. Now we have a solid, workable plan. **Read on. Take this simple plan, and let's save this**

nation for our children and grandchildren.

Speaking of parties, you'll notice that you won't find the R word or the D words in this book. It's not about party. It's about principles. The Founders' basic beliefs were libertarian in nature, though they didn't call them that. In this sense you could say that my approach is libertarian, without allegiance to the modern Libertarian Party. Like the thousands of patriots who show up at tea parties, we're fed up with partisan politics. We just want our country and our liberty back. We've reached the limit of our patience and our hope in either major party, and we're stepping over the carcasses of the parties with new blood and good old-fashioned common sense.

Now a word to incumbents in Congress: No matter which political party you are in, your time of ignoring the Constitution, the rule of law, and common sense is just about up. We have a representative republic, not a democracy. You are supposed to uphold the Constitution, not the mob. If the flag on the cover of this book frightens you, it should. And the more you see that flag image, the more earnestly you should be looking for another job. I don't speak for all tea partiers. But I think I can safely say that I express the outrage of millions of Americans who have been ignored by the major parties and run over by big government. We're not taking it any more. If you ignore or disparage us, we'll only grow stronger and more determined and you won't know what hit you next November. But if you sincerely listen, and agree with at least half of this book, come join us. It's time to speak up. It's time to vote. It's time to get back to America's founding principles and values!

I'm looking forward to a return to the rule of law, where the Constitution is respected and adhered to at all levels, including the courts; where people's property is not taken by government decree; where states are once again sovereign and have freedom from federal manipulation; where individuals respect and support strong, yet humble leaders, because those leaders are there to serve their fellow citizens rather than themselves.

But do you know what I look forward to most? I can't wait for the day when government is put in its place and individuals are once again self-reliant...the day when my fellow citizens find it unnecessary to either idolize or demonize their leaders, because government will have become mostly *irrelevant* to their lives. A free people with a moral government don't have to worry about all the details of legislation. They are free to go about their business, building, expanding, and realizing their dreams—trusting that their representatives are living up to their oaths. Honest representatives of a free people don't spend their time scheming ways to raise taxes and then jockeying for the right to spend the people's money on their pet projects, sure to endear them to constituents and solidify their power. They spend their time looking for ways to increase freedom, undo onerous laws, and make government a smaller and more efficient servant.

I am aware of the huge threats we face from illegal immigration; the nuclear ambitions of Iran, North Korea, and others; drug abuse and the culture war in the United States; the rising tide of economic and political unrest in various countries; and terrorism from radical Islam and drug cartels, among others. In fact, events are moving so quickly today that I will not be surprised if some terrorist event larger than 9/11 occurs before this book is in bookstores. Don't let circumstances and events scare you off from this noble cause. If we are not vigilant, the media will do everything they can to make you think that some other issue is more important that this. They will be wrong. **None of the other threats we face is more dangerous than the lack of personal responsibility and integrity we face in our population, in our media, and in our elected representatives. Without personal integrity and responsibility, freedom cannot exist.**

It is with a great sense of gratitude and optimism that I offer this book to the people who will take up the challenge to revive the

American dream of freedom. I believe our Founding Fathers' spirit of liberty can rise again. I believe that the sacrifices of thousands before us were not made in vain, but will live on if we persevere in spreading the true wealth—the American dream, the desire to live free—to as many Americans as possible.

One word of caution before we go on: Throughout this book, you'll see many references to God and to Jesus. Please rest assured that you do not need to be a Christian or to believe in any particular form of God in order to embrace American values and principles. It was part of the genius of our Founding Fathers that adherence to any specific creed was not necessary for citizenship. The Constitution they devised allowed for a broad range of beliefs and unbelief. But, since America was settled mostly by Christians who came here to escape persecution, we are the heirs of a strong legacy of Christian doctrine and influence. I hope you'll set aside any prejudice you may have against Christianity as a religion. It is not my intent, nor is it within my power,[5] to convince anyone of the truth of Jesus Christ. However, no honest student of American history can deny His influence on our founding and our Constitution. **My hope is that, no matter what spiritual beliefs you may have, you will find the wisdom of the Founders here, and like Washington in the snow, you will pray that Almighty God will intervene on behalf of our nation and its future.**

If you are already on board with the movement to save America from its government, I hope you'll see this book as a resource to pass along, especially to potential or incumbent congresspersons and everyone you know who votes. When your grandchildren ask what you did in the Revolution of 2010-2012, you will be able to say that you did your part to spread this wealth and pass this ammunition!

C. Jesse Duke
June 2009

Chapter One

Was It Just a Dream?

"Liberty must at all hazards be supported. We have a right to it, derived from our Maker. But if we had not, our fathers have earned and bought it for us, at the expense of their ease, their estates, their pleasure, and their blood."

— John Adams

"This will be the best security for maintaining our liberties: A nation of well-informed men who have been taught to know and prize the rights which God has given them cannot be enslaved. It is in the religion of ignorance that tyranny begins."

— Benjamin Franklin

On a muggy August day in 1963, Dr. Martin Luther King, Jr. stood on the steps of the Lincoln Memorial and delivered one of the most famous speeches in American history. I quote it in part here to emphasize that the American dream is one of freedom and equality of opportunity based on faith in God's ultimate justice as the embodiment of Truth:

I say to you today, my friends, so even though we face the difficulties of today and tomorrow, I still have a dream. It is a dream deeply rooted in the American dream. I have a dream that one day this nation will rise up and live out the true meaning of its creed: "We hold these truths to be self-evident: that all men are created equal." I have a dream that one day on the red hills of Georgia the sons of former slaves and the sons of former slave owners will be able to sit down together at the table of brotherhood. I have a dream that one day even the state of Mississippi, a state sweltering with the heat of injustice, sweltering with the heat of oppression, will be transformed into an oasis of freedom and justice. I have a dream that my four little children will one day live in a nation where they will not be judged by the color of their skin but by the content of their character…

I have a dream today.

And when this happens, when we allow freedom to ring, when we let it ring from every village and every hamlet, from every state and every city, we will be able to speed up that day when all of God's children, black men and white men, Jews and Gentiles, Protestants and Catholics, will be able to join hands and sing in the words of the old Negro spiritual, "Free at last! Free at last! Thank God Almighty, we are free at last!"

Many today think of the American Dream as material success. Although prosperity has certainly been possible for many as a *result* of the American Dream, it is not the dream itself. Historian and writer, James Truslow Adams, coined the phrase "American Dream" in his 1931 book, *The Epic of America*. In it he said:

"The American Dream is that dream of a land in which life should be better and richer and fuller for everyone, with

*opportunity for each **according to ability or achievement**... It is not a dream of motor cars and high wages merely, but a dream of social order in which each man and each woman shall **be able to attain to the fullest stature of which they are innately capable**, and be recognized by others for what they are, **regardless** of the fortuitous circumstances of birth or position."*[1] [Emphasis mine.]

Throughout history, men and women have longed to be free—to set their own course and to live life to the fullest by pursuing ideas, adventures, and aspirations of their own choosing. But human beings are not naturally inclined to be gracious toward one other. So, it has taken warlords, kings, tyrants, governors, emperors, and the like to wield power over people's lives for common purposes, good and bad. While under the control of such leaders, the only way to gain sovereignty over one's life was to separate from society and live alone. In such a state, the individual is vulnerable to the elements and to wild animals and predatory humans.

So, we learned to form communities for mutual protection, and to combine our efforts to supply ourselves with food, drink, shelter, and other necessities of life. Life is physically easier in community, but community presents its own problems. Alone, an individual has only to deal with himself and his own survival. In relation to others, even just one other, problems arise because of self-interest.

Understanding the nature of human self-interest, men began to use it as a means of supplying mutual needs. Because of our own self-interest we are motivated to work, build, and create. Knowing that community offers the most advantage against the elements and that mutual self-interest could sustain them, people began seeking to find the best way to live with each other. Tribes, kingdoms, democracies, republics, and other such forms of community have come and gone as the experiment in ways to organize societies has progressed. Most forms of government were begun, sustained, and eventually ended by bloodshed.

It was only after the Protestant Reformation occurred in Europe, 400 years ago, that people began to see *virtue* as a foundation for governmental organization. The Reformation taught, for the first time, that men and women each had a personal individual responsibility toward God and each other. It also revealed to millions of people that God not only cared about how they lived, but that He loved them and wanted them to love each other. Jesus Christ was not just a person in ancient history, but a living Spirit who could and did transform lives from within. It was this awakening, more than anything else, that awakened the longing for freedom to work and worship in their self-chosen ways, and to be accountable to no one but this living God.

America was founded upon the principle that all men are created equal. This was a fundamental Christian principle, never before expressed in a collection of individuals. It was this principle that gave our Founders the conviction that all men have the right to participate in their own government. Although it took many more years and struggles for men to understand the extent of this principle, as in the case of voting rights for negroes, and then women, it was a principle that would not be suppressed forever.

Along with the right to participate in government comes the duty to educate oneself about the issues of the day so that you can make correctly informed decisions. Because of our biases, based on experience, we don't all come to the same conclusions from the same information. **Only by mutual agreement in advance to "agree to disagree" can we make the necessary laws to govern ourselves in peace.** Thus, we establish and live by a "rule of law" for self-government, outside of which, no arbitrary person or power can act with impunity. We each surrender some of our wants in order to have a reasonable, harmonious existence. It was this divinely inspired understanding that enabled the formation of the United States. Many called the United States an "experiment" in self-government. But it is no longer an experiment. Self-government has proven to be a sound psychological, social, and economic success, and it will continue to be as long as it is sustained by vigilance against those who would destroy it. We have dropped our vigilance and the enemy has come in through the front gate. Now what are we to do about it? Do we roll over and die or do we fight to regain freedom for ourselves and future generations?

The modern image of the American dream, since approximately the beginning of the industrial era, is one of material prosperity—a house, a car, a certain number of children, and a life of material comforts. For many, these have been life-goals. For many, including those who variously and historically have found themselves in minority groups, this version of the American Dream has been elusive and even discouraging. With little or no hope to achieve material success, many have fallen into the trap of self-limitation instead of rising above the tide of prejudicial ignorance.

Nothing is wrong with wanting or having material possessions. They represent physical security, as long as we have a government that acts in such a way as to protect them for us. But I submit that this vision of the American dream is shortsighted and eventually destructive, because it causes us to lose sight of the real and highest dream: freedom from coercion by any other human beings. When the government that is supposed to protect our rights begins itself to be a barrier to our freedom, and to coerce "compliance" with onerous or unnecessary laws and regulations, we tend to get rebellious—or at least some of us do.

To live in peace and safety and to have the freedom to pursue our individual dreams is the American Dream. It is individual self-interest in freedom that has enabled America to continue for as long as it has. We each have a self-interest in prosperity and security for our children and grandchildren. By each individual pursuing his or her dreams, the dream would endure. And we have always assumed that in America, the dream would be assured, as long as we have a strong military. Remember the way we reacted to the attacks of 9/11/01? We were outraged. We marshaled all the forces of our government to destroy the enemy and protect against any further attack. We are relentless in our defense against foreign enemies. But we seem to be powerless against the forces within our own government that are causing far worse damage than any terrorist could inflict.

Our own government has transformed us into a debtor nation. On September 19, 2008, our national debt was $9,684,016,631,715.87. In March of 2009, it became over eleven trillion dollars. That's a one-and-a-half-trillion dollar increase in five months! This was all done because we were told that we had to bail out some "troubled assets" of big financial institutions that were deemed "too big to fail." These troubled assets were, at their core, derived from the government-enabled practice of lending money to people who were unlikely to pay it back!

The lending decisions these banks made were bad, and they should have suffered the consequences of their bad decisions—not for punishment, but because it is the natural order, the way of the free market. People and institutions learn and improve when they are allowed to suffer the consequences of their decisions, good and bad. But government, the Great Enabler, jumped in to save the day.

Government has spent beyond its means ever since the Roosevelt administration. **The fault lies with Congress, which controls the purse strings of government. This means that the fault belongs with the American people for not voting more intelligently for their congresspersons.** We can blame Congress as much as we want, but we have to remember in the end that Congress is only a reflection of our decisions at the ballot box.

Was It Just a Dream?

Our Founders knew that freedom can be fragile, and they knew the only way to maintain it is by remaining aware of, and defending it from, any threats against it. Thomas Jefferson told us, *"The price of freedom is eternal vigilance."* The Founders' generation had more sense than us, because they came from a background of coercive governments. Patrick Henry said, *"The Constitution is not an instrument for the government to restrain the people, it is an instrument for the people to restrain the government—lest it come to dominate our lives and interests."*

Like people living on a fault line or in a hurricane zone, we have become used to the protracted freedom they gave us, and this is where we are vulnerable. We tend to think that it will just go on and on without much maintenance or effort. Every now and then, like on a 9/11, we get a jolt of reality where we can see it could very well be lost. We rouse from our slumber and fight off the enemy, only to go right back to sleep again.

It's difficult to admit that we are under assault by the very government we have put into place. We have looked the other way for many years, allowing government to grow beyond its Constitutional limits. We have pretended that it isn't really happening. We have even voted for hope and change, with the hope that someone would make a real change. But the only change we get, every time, is more and more government. In the case of our current Congress and President, we've got it times ten!

Although we cannot force others to participate in the protection of their own freedoms, it is our duty to inform them of the dangers we face if our freedoms are not protected. We sustain the freedom-contract by education.

Public education has dropped the ball, and many of our fellow citizens do not know where we came from. They do not know that our forefathers were divinely inspired to come here to establish a place where all men are equal—not equally gifted or equally challenged, but equally endowed with the rights to life, liberty, and the opportunity to pursue their God-given dreams. Patrick Henry said, *"When people forget God, tyrants forge their chains."* They escaped the tyranny of kings, but we have slowly been making a tyrant of government itself. This book is about reclaiming the freedom that government has usurped.

I began writing this book in 2007, and I have tried to keep up with the societal changes that have occurred since then, not the least of which were the outrageous bailouts and the election of 2008. It has been impossible to keep up with the pace of events. Besides, there is not enough space is in this book to list the countless mind-boggling changes that have taken place since 2007. I am grateful, therefore, for the serendipitous release of three important books that have been published in recent months that do go into detail about these events, their origins, and their meanings.

These books are, **Mark Levin's**, *Liberty and Tyranny*, **Glenn Beck's**, *Common Sense*, **and Jim Demint's**, *Saving Freedom*. It seems all four of us were writing about preserving liberty at the same time. It won't surprise me if more similar books and audiobooks are released in the near future. There cannot be too many. We are not in competition to sell books. We are all about spreading the true wealth of America that has been ignored for so long. Each of us has a unique perspective and valuable insights as to what can be done to preserve freedom for future generations. These three books are listed in Appendix A, along with such indispensable resources as the thirty-year-old history book, *The 5,000 Year Leap*. How grateful I am to all of these authors for their work, their passion, and their insights! Unfortunately, all of them came to my attention after I had finished most of this book, so I didn't have a chance to quote them. The striking thing is that the theme running through all of these books is that the greatest threat to American freedom is coming from within, from our fellow citizens in government who do not respect the original intent of the Constitution. I could not sound an alarm loud enough to emphasize this!

If the American Dream is to live in peace and safety so that we may pursue our individual aspirations, why have we allowed our very own government to grow so big as to be a threat to that dream? I am thoroughly convinced that we allowed it because we willingly gave up esteeming the truth of God in exchange for the lies of men.[2] Rather than believing that we were created in the image of a creative God, with our own God-given abilities, we decided that some people were simply incapable of pursuing their own dreams, or even having dreams. So we allowed government to forcibly take property from some to support others whom we deemed not capable. On the surface it seems compassionate, but at its root is arrogance and condescension.

Benjamin Franklin said, *"The Constitution only gives people the right to pursue happiness. You have to catch it yourself."* By patronizing our fellow citizens under the guise of "helping" them, we have taken away their fundamental dignity.[3] Anyone who has ever had a goal or pursued a dream of any sort can attest that it is the pursuit of the goal that has brought happiness to their lives. Most successful people look back at the struggles in their lives as the best times of their lives, because it gave them purpose and hope. When we are using our God-given abilities to pursue worthy goals, we are exercising our freedom in the way God intended.[4]

The pursuit of a personally chosen, worthwhile goal is empowering, uplifting, and full of internal rewards. We were designed to struggle toward the dreams that God puts in us. Pity the man who has no goal. Pity still the man or woman who has aspirations without acknowledging a higher source or help than his own strength. He or she will inevitably step on other people to attain the goal. Or worse yet, he or she may blame others or "the system" when up against immovable obstacles.

The American dream is spelled out in the Declaration of

Independence. It is a dream of freedom to struggle toward a goal of one's own choosing, according to one's own conscience, without the hindrance of onerous and senseless laws. It is the security of knowing that life is sacred and that fellow persons hold this same value, and we and our families will be safe as we pursue our goals. The American dream would not even be possible without political liberty, and that is what is at stake today. When that fails, we can forget about the dream.

I make a huge assumption while writing this book. I assume that most Americans are aware of current federal government attempts to nationalize (gain control of) huge segments of our economy under the guise of "saving" it. I also assume that rumblings in the counter-culture are coming from patriots who are both ashamed of having let government get this far, and angry that it no longer respects the Constitution. They want to do something but they are frustrated that any opposition to the prevailing powers that be will be portrayed by the elite media as extremists.

Let me deflect that here and now. First of all, there is not much to be gained by trying to get elite and arrogant media types to see or report the truth, as we saw during the April 15th, 2009 Tea Party reporting. They will shill for government because government is power. Second, we may as well face it, we *are* extremists, as extreme as the Founders who fought for our independence, gained it, then put together a brilliant Constitution. Let's not doubt that the elites in government or the media will come up with any demonizing term that their focus groups approve, but we should wear the extremist label with pride, because it will take extreme courage to face down the forces of sophistry, shallow elitism, and partisan politics. We cannot let that stop the effort to downsize government. Too much is at stake to allow a little name-calling to deter us.

We are in a war that is both cultural and political that has its roots in the spiritual and moral. The only way to win this war is nonviolently, at the ballot box. The weapons of war are prayer and education. **Beware of anyone who would resort to or advocate violence. We'd have a heck of a time ever stopping it. Besides, violence only invites more government, the very thing we want less of!**

More is involved in fighting a non-violent war than just rounding up enough votes to make a political change. Politics are merely a reflection of the character of individuals. Hearts and minds must be changed, and that is basically God's business. Pray that God Himself will cause all people, especially those in power, to begin to see the folly of reliance on government. Pray as if it were all up to God, but act as if it were all up to you to learn about, and to educate others, on the principles of individual liberty and responsibility, self-reliance, and free markets.

Only in these ways can we "overthrow" the government that is no longer of or for the individual. Since we cannot change anyone else's heart and mind, we must simply set an example so that when God begins to change hearts, others will know what self-ownership looks like. We must, as individuals, examine ourselves[5] and be sure that we are not relying on government for anything but what it was designed for—to secure our rights to life and liberty—and to get out of the way so that we are free to pursue our individual dreams.

When we allow government to take our liberty, we all lose. We must all hang together and be vigilant against government takeovers of private companies, banks, health care, education, and all other aspects of private life. You may think of government as a savior, but I guarantee you, whenever government does something for you, it takes freedom from you.

The loss of freedom has been slow and gradual up until now. But just look around. You can see government nannyism everywhere. Just look at the tag on a electrical cord, a pillow, a bucket, or a can of paint. Listen to the public service ads on the radio warning us against everything from wearing a life jacket when we go out in a boat, to wearing sunscreen, to child immunizations, etc. The list is endless and embarrassing. Pretty soon we will all have to post signs on our bedroom walls to warn us that getting out of bed in the morning can be hazardous. Something may go wrong today! The more we allow government to do *for* us, the more we allow government to take *from* us. Do you not see it? How can you be free when every decision you make must take into account what government will do for you or to you?

Government does not belong in every area of our lives. But since we have forgotten our values and principles, we have allowed it in. Our task now is to get it back out of our lives by restoring the values and principles that made America the last, best hope of mankind. The next chapter spells out the values and principles we need to embrace as individuals and to teach to our sons and daughters, so that we can return America to its former, and future, strength and goodness.

Chapter Two

American Values and Founding Principles

"Educate and inform the whole mass of the people ... They are the only sure reliance for the preservation of our Liberty."

— Thomas Jefferson

"Happy is the man who finds wisdom, and the man who gains understanding." — Proverbs 3:13

In a letter to James Warren in 1779, Samuel Adams said, *"A general dissolution of principles and manners will more surely overthrow the liberties of America than the whole force of the common enemy. While the people are virtuous they cannot be subdued; but when once they lose their virtue, they will be ready to surrender their liberties to the first external or internal invader."*

Our "internal invaders" are elected and appointed officials who do not adhere to these principles and values. Mr. Adams exhorts us to find representatives who will live up to the principles and values we hold dear—not just talk about them: *"If ever time should come, when vain and aspiring men shall possess the highest seats in Government, our country will stand in need of its experienced patriots to prevent its ruin."*

Mr. Adams also tells us: *"He therefore is the truest friend to the liberty of his country who tries most to promote its virtue, and who, so far as his power and influence extend, will not suffer a man to be chosen into any office of power and trust who is not a wise and virtuous man ... The sum of all is, if we would most truly enjoy this gift of Heaven, let us become a virtuous people."*

Adherence to values and principles is for everyone, not just leaders. In fact, we cannot discern wisdom and virtue in those who would lead us unless we ourselves are wise and virtuous. This does not mean we have to be perfect, but that we make an honest effort to seek wisdom and virtue.[1]

A value is a fundamental truth, natural law, a doctrine, or a motivating force upon which principles are based. For example, we value life, so our basic principles on the absolute right that every human being has to exist. Every law should descend from this basic value. A strong national defense, and personal right to defend oneself and others come from this value. Unfortunately sometimes this includes taking predator's lives in defense of innocent lives.

We value freedom and private property, so one of our principles is that no one has the right to take what belongs to someone else.[2] Property and freedom are linked together because without absolute ownership of oneself, one's thoughts, and one's creations, there is no freedom. Freedom, by definition, is the freedom to use one's property as one sees fit.

Our Declaration of Independence says that we have certain "inalienable" rights, meaning that they cannot be legally taken from us. These are life, liberty, and the pursuit of happiness. These are "among" the rights that we value, but they are only some of our natural, God-given rights. Alexander Hamilton said, *"The sacred rights of mankind are not to be rummaged for among old parchments or musty records. They are written, as with a sunbeam, in the whole volume of human nature, by the hand of the Divinity itself, and can never be erased or obscured by mortal power."*

Even if you don't believe in a personal God who would bestow such rights, you are still heir to those rights. Natural rights can be said to be in the "nature" of things—it's just common sense, the way things are. Even if you don't believe there is a God, you have to believe in a natural order, because you are a part of it.

The Bible was the source of many of the values and principles that the Founders and early settlers of America held dear. The Bible was considered to be the ultimate authority in human affairs. This does not mean that the Bible established these values and principles, but that the Bible is merely a document that *states* those values and principles. Other documents state them also, in different ways. For example, *"You shall not murder,"*³ is a Biblical tenet; yet, even people who have never read that commandment have a natural understanding, an intuitive knowledge, that killing is "wrong." You'll find statements supporting this in legal and religious documents all over he world. This moral "code" of the value of human life is written on the human heart. Your understanding of the origin of liberty may be completely different from mine, and yet we have an unspoken agreement that you are entitled to your view and I, mine, and we don't have to kill each other because of our differences. We do this because we value life.

We do have a problem, however, when some do not accept our values. Yet, attempting to force free individuals to value our values is oxymoronic. **In order for a value or principle to be adhered to, it has to be freely chosen.** This is one of the dilemmas faced by the Founding Fathers. They dealt with it by persuasive writings, sermons, and speeches. They knew that honest, freedom-loving individuals could be persuaded by common sense and logic. However, they also knew that many people would choose not to embrace certain values. That's where the law comes in. Those who do not freely choose to adhere to common values and principles are subject to correction in various degrees—from warnings, to fines, to prisons, all the way to the death penalty.

The values Americans have always held dear, even though we have been largely unable to live up to all of them, are available to everyone. Our values are the sanctity of life, physical and political liberty, and private property (which includes the property of our thoughts). Our principles are based on these values. I list some of those principles below. When we speak of values and principles, it is not as though we are speaking of things unattainable. They all are attainable, but we must choose to work toward them. The religious freedom that our forefathers sought when they came to this country included the freedom to choose and to practice these principles as they saw fit.

Personal responsibility. This is the very first and foundational principle of America. Without it, there is chaos and an absence of freedom. When each individual takes responsibility for his or her actions, his or her failures, his or her sustenance, not blaming others for personal problems, then everyone's space is respected, and harmony exists. We are not responsible for anyone else,[4] although we may choose to help others in their efforts to provide for themselves. This matter of choice, of free will, is crucial. If we are free to do or not do for others, then we allow them the same freedom. This mutual "live and let live" attitude is our silent code. No one else is responsible to provide for me or bail me out of my circumstances. Conversely, I am not responsible for anyone else's success or failure in life. The exception, of course, applies to children. Parents are always responsible for what their minor children do or don't do.

Self-reliance. The early pioneers ventured out into the wilderness with nothing but the clothes on their backs and a few basic tools. As they settled the land, they raised their children to have the same sense of self-capability, ingenuity, and perseverance. Then *their* children passed it on, and so on... It was a foregone conclusion, up until the middle of the 20th century, that each individual was to take care of himself. It was also a foregone fact of life that no one can be completely "self"-sufficient. "Self" always included family, friends, and neighbors. No one would have considered *government* as a place to go for help, except in matters of legal dispute or when police or military protection was required and available.

Private property. Respect for each other's stuff is another sign of personal maturity. Even God tells us not to "covet" another's property.[5] Envy is an ugly thing. And when it is institutionalized, as in a political party, it is even uglier and more dangerous. What people don't realize is that when we do not respect the property of others, it degrades us and erects a barrier to our own prosperity. As long as I think you shouldn't have something I don't have (and make no mistake, this is what class envy does), then I am powerless to attain my own property. Respect for private property is a fundamental duty of each individual, and, as such, it should be for the state, too. As you will see in the next chapter, private property includes not just physical items you own, but your ideas, dreams, inventions, and even your own self.

In 1792, James Madison, the man responsible for writing much of the Constitution, wrote an essay on "Property" in *The National Gazette*. In the article, he defines property in several ways:

> "This term in its particular application means 'that dominion which one man claims and exercises over the external things of the world, in exclusion of every other individual. In its larger and juster meaning, it embraces every thing to which a man may attach a value and have a right; and which leaves to every one else the like advantage. In the former sense, a man's land, or merchandize, or money is called his property. In the latter sense, a man has property in his opinions and the free communication of them. He has a

property of peculiar value in his religious opinions, and in the profession and practice dictated by them. He has property very dear to him in the safety and liberty of his person. He has an equal property in the free use of his faculties and free choice of the objects on which to employ them. In a word, as a man is said to have a right to his property, he may be equally said to have a property in his rights.

"*Where an excess of power prevails, property of no sort is duly respected. No man is safe in his opinions, his person, his faculties or his possessions.*

"*Government is instituted to protect property of every sort; as well that which lies in the various rights of individuals, as that which the term particularly expresses. This being the end of government, that alone is a just government, which impartially secures to every man, whatever is his own.*

"*According to this standard of merit, the praise of affording a just security to property, should be sparingly bestowed on a government which, however scrupulously guarding the possessions of individuals, does not protect them in the enjoyment and communication of their opinions, in which they have an equal, and in the estimation of some, a more valuable property.*

"*More sparingly should this praise be allowed to a government, where a man's religious rights are violated by penalties, or lettered by tests, or taxed by a hierarchy. Conscience is the most sacred of all property; other property depending in part on positive law, the exercise of that, being a natural and inalienable right. To guard a man's house as his castle, to pay public and enforce private debts with the most exact faith, can give no title to invade a man's conscience which is more sacred than his castle, or to withhold from it that debt of protection, for which the public faith is pledged,* by the very nature and original conditions of the social pact."

Many people do not believe in the concept of private property today, as evidenced by the widespread support for socialism. But, take their MP3 players or their cars, and suddenly they'll discover what it means to respect private property. In the next chapter, I'll explain the foundational nature of private property and why all economies—personal and national—are based on this fundamental natural right.

The Rule of Law. Man is born with a sense of justice.[6] We don't like it when wrongdoing is not punished, and right deeds are not rewarded. No man or woman, no matter how exalted in the eyes of other men or women, is beyond the law. Even if the President commits a crime, he can be prosecuted for it. The ultimate law is the Constitution, and all other laws are measured against it (or should be). This is why it is so crucial that our "lawmakers" respect the Constitution when considering legislation. Of course, we have drifted from this principle as a nation, mainly because we as citizens have not been vigilant to hold our representatives accountable to their oath to *"defend the Constitution against all enemies foreign and domestic[7],"* including themselves.

Limited Government. In our Constitution, we gave government a monopoly on the legitimate use of force so that it could protect every citizen's right to life, liberty, and property. Its proper role is to defend us from enemies within and beyond our borders, to protect us from anyone who would take away our liberties, and to defend our rights to our private property. When government fails in its duty, we have a responsibility to defend these rights against any infringement, whether it be from criminals or from government. Theoretically, *we are* our government, because we elect fellow citizens to uphold these rights. And yet, time and circumstances have served to grow government into a monstrosity that must be right-sized. George Washington said, *"Government is a good servant, but an evil master."* We have allowed it to become a master, simply by allowing it to become so big. We have asked it to meet needs that we should be meeting ourselves, as individuals. Now it is our duty to prune it back to its right size, not only for ourselves, but for future generations.

"Right size" does not necessarily have a measurement such as dollars spent or taxed per person, nor does it necessarily mean representation based on population. But it does mean the size necessary to perform legitimate Constitutional functions, and nothing more. By this measure, we would have had no trillion-dollar "stimulus" packages, or multi-billion dollar bailouts of big businesses. Nor would we be giving billions of taxpayer dollars to various private organizations, such as ACORN, to do the bidding of a political party. There is not room to list the ways in which taxpayers' money is used unconstitutionally. Needless to say, a right sized government would have no business doing any such thing.

<u>The Constitution is Primary.</u> This does not mean that we worship the document, but that we uphold its original intent and defend it against all attempts to ignore it or to impose meanings that it does not contain. The Constitution itself contains provisions for legally changing it. Because of this, we have no problem with attempts at legal amendments. In fact, I suggest some later in this book. What we have a problem with is political distortions of the intent of the Constitution's writers. Much of their personal and political writings shed light on their original intent. For example, some moderns have come to believe that the First Amendment's clause stating, *"Congress shall make no law respecting an establishment of religion,"* means that no religious activity should take place around anything that has to do with government. But history shows that church services were held in the very building where Congress met, and the writings of the Founders are rife with admonitions against straying from Biblical precepts. Congress even funded missionaries to Native Americans and the printing of Bibles. So, in

American Values and Founding Principles

this example, we see the original intent was not to exclude religion from government, but that government would not authorize a *specified* state religion, such as the Church of England.

Irrespective of many frivolous claims, religious writings and symbols in or near government buildings, schools, or documents do not constitute government sanction, but rather government acknowledgment of the original intent of the Founders, as spelled out in the First Amendment. In many such ways we allow the Constitution to be the law of the land.

Integrity in government. We believe that those who serve at all levels of government should be held to a standard of integrity such that when any violation of the public trust is committed, the offending public officials should be fired or required to resign with no monetary compensation. The election or appointment to public office is a privilege and a duty, and all office holders should remember that they work for the people and must be guided in their duties by the people's Constitution.[8] Period. We should be looking for leaders among us who have already shown integrity such as this.

Truth in Journalism. In our history, we have always had those sleazy journalists who put a "spin" on the news so that people would come to the conclusions those "reporters" or their bosses wanted. But in our modern world, spin has become an art that is so widespread, it is difficult to believe *any* news reporting. Watching the distortions some in news media go through to support big government and its proponents can sometimes be entertaining, but most of the time it's maddening! People want the truth. Many major newspapers and television outlets have dwindling customer bases today as the consumers of news find more reliable sources of news. We can't make a law saying that journalists must tell the truth, but we can exercise our right to seek truth elsewhere. The Internet is full of both reliable and unreliable sources, and that is how it should be.

Individuals are responsible to do their "homework" to discover the truth in any situation. Truthful information won't be found in sound bites or cute slogans. It will only be found by honest seekers who demand thorough and unbiased information from media. The free market will sort out journalists as consumers demand more honesty in reporting, especially political reporting. Wouldn't life be so much better for everyone if those who call themselves journalists would simply report the facts and nothing but the facts?[9]

Clean Elections. We believe in the right of all citizens over the age of eighteen, regardless of race, religion, or gender, to cast secret ballots for the candidates of their choice, as long as they are legally registered and eligible to vote. We also believe that the voter has the responsibility to be informed not only on the issues of the day, but *especially in basic economics and history.* Voters should be required to register in advance of any election and to prove positively that they are citizens. But we do not believe that tax money should be used to recruit, encourage, or educate voters, as is being done now. All of those things can and should be done by private means. We do believe that government should be unbiased in monitoring election processes so that fraudulent voting or fraudulent exclusion of voters does not occur. It is all of our responsibility, as private citizens, to ensure against election fraud.

Strong National and Personal Defense. Without a strong national defense, we would have no place to exercise our freedoms; therefore, we would have no freedoms. It's as simple as that. The way to maintain peace in the world is to be constantly prepared for war. This is not something to neglect or ignore. We must insist that Congress fund and maintain a strong and ready military. We must also insist that waste and corruption be taken out of the system of military spending.

On a smaller scale, but no less important, is the individual's right to defend himself or herself, their property, and family from any threats to peace and safety. Congress should make no law respecting the rights of responsible individuals to own and use deadly weapons.[10] States should also not infringe on this fundamental right, except to exclude those who have proven to be irresponsible toward the rule of law.

Common Courtesy. One largely unspoken value that Americans hold dear is the principle that comes from the Bible, *"Do unto others as you would have them do unto you."*[11] Minimally, this means simply not doing or saying things that would harm other people.[12] Of course no one can live up to this all the time, but we at least hold it as a standard of conduct. Traditionally, Americans have gone out of their way to help each other because of this golden rule of life. We used to have barn raisings and a tradition of neighbor helping neighbor, and in many areas of the country you will find this principle at work every day. As our cities get more and more crowded it's harder for people to take the time to be kind to each other, but it is still possible and preferable to the alternative. As a rule, Americans show respect for each other. It's mostly in the pop culture media that disrespect is prevalent, mainly because the purveyors of pop culture are usually the young and immature seeking to impress each other.[13]

Free Markets. Without the ability and freedom to personally decide whether to buy or sell something at a price of our own choosing, a market is not free. When we choose to pay a particular price for something, we will have made a personal decision based on comparison to other prices, proximity of the item, quality, personal relationship to the seller, or any number of factors. It is our choice. This freedom is what gives anything a "market value." When government imposes restrictions on what can be bought or sold and at what price, the market is no longer free. This inevitably leads to higher prices and less freedom for everyone.

Private charity. Most Americans have traditionally believed in and supported non-governmental charities to help each other. From neighbor-to-neighbor helping hands, to large and small religious initiatives to help the poor, Americans have always been ready and eager to reach out to those in legitimate need. We believe the government has no responsibility or right to use tax monies for charitable reasons, and that it should neither interfere with private charities nor compete with them to "help" the needy.[14]

Income is Private. Besides being bad manners to ask or tell another's income, an individual's income is no one else's business. Government should have no business whatsoever either knowing or claiming any portion of the income of private citizens.

Freedom to worship or not worship. The First Amendment protects us from government-sponsored religion. It does not prevent individuals from expressing their religious beliefs in private or public. As a culture, we have traditionally respected people's rights to expressions of faith, no matter how strange they may appear to us. Government has no legitimate role in either judging what is "religious" or not, or regulating any form of expression of faith. Also, by secularizing American society, government is establishing the religion of government, and thereby is in violation of the First Amendment.

Chapter Three

Says Who?

"Our Constitution is designed only for a moral and religious people. It is wholly inadequate for any other."

— John Adams

"How much better it is to get wisdom than gold! And to get understanding is better than silver."

— Proverbs 16:16

The only reason we are aware of the principles and values outlined in the previous chapter is that the Founding Fathers were steeped in philosophies of men like Plato, Aristotle, Cicero, Augustine, Locke, and Rousseau, in addition to the precepts of the Bible. They also had the experience of living under tyrannical government. Most people in the America of the 1700s, even the "uneducated," were at least aware of Biblical wisdom. It was part of the culture. We are heirs to that culture, whether we like it or not.

This does not mean that all wisdom comes from the Bible, but that God *is* Himself wisdom.[1] God's wisdom is made known to humans through the Bible, but God also gave man the capacity to discern wisdom through the natural world[2] because He created man in His image.[3] This is why you will find wisdom that corresponds to Biblical wisdom in various other religious traditions throughout the world. Don't assume my references to the Bible are "support" for my statements about the origin of man or anything else. God was revealing Himself through nature long before *any* scriptures of *any* religion were written down. The facts don't need "support." It's really just the opposite—the scientific facts "support" what God has already said. Isn't it a nice coincidence that modern scientists are finding that what the Bible says is true? It sure will save a lot of time explaining God to future generations who will have even more scientific evidence than we do now!

The extent to which freedom has existed throughout history is the extent to which true wisdom has been present. Up until about the 1960s, most Americans understood that America had a God-ordained beginning and destiny, and that it was up to its citizens to fulfill that destiny by adhering to traditional values and principles. This is the main reason we are losing our freedoms today—many have simply exchanged the wisdom of God for the foolishness of man.[4] But the Founding Fathers knew that freedom could only be sustained by a religious and moral people.[5]

If you don't believe in a providential beginning to America, then you may find it hard to see how the character of each individual will determine the future of the nation. Sad to say, the idea that we are endowed with values and rights from God is foreign, and even silly, to some today. Many, including far too many in government, have bought into the ideas of Darwin and others like him, and logic and common sense have been abandoned in the name of "science."[6]

Now widely taught in government schools is the theory that man originated from animals that evolved from single-cell organisms, etc.—totally excluding even the possibility of an intelligent design. I have never met a young person who actually believes this, but I've met many who regurgitate it, because it is easier to just go along with the teachers and textbooks than it is to think deeply about why they don't believe it. This sort of intellectual laziness is the cause of many social problems today. I submit that this laziness is the origin of our current headlong rush into socialism.

If we all evolved from a primordial swamp, which just *happened* into existence billions of years ago, then humans aren't more than mere super-animals. And if we're animals, then all we have to aspire to is our instincts and desires, simply taking what we want or need. If we're animals, we have no purpose except just to survive, have a good time, and die. Life would have no transcendent meaning beyond that, and therefore we have no reason to seek to do good or rise higher in either the moral or spiritual realms. Many people believe in a godless evolution theory of origins, because it eliminates the need for ethical and moral considerations. What works and what doesn't, what feels good and what doesn't, are the only criteria for judgment.

Just as Biblical understanding was part of the prevailing culture around the time of the founding of America, relativism is a large part of our culture today. Relativism is the theory that all values and judgments are "relative" to the context of any given situation, culture, or person. A majority today believes that to hold anything to be absolutely true (such as the God of the Bible) is ignorant or "intolerant" of other people, because we all have a right to our own beliefs. This idea refutes itself, because it is saying that only relativism is true, which would make it an absolute truth.

The fact is that God Himself *is* diversity. In the entire universe, no two creations are exactly alike. The stance of absolute Truth is that this Truth created everything with His own purposes in mind for each thing and person He created. Everything and everyone has ultimate meaning and value. Just as the earth revolves around the sun, the entire universe and all of the diversity of life revolves around, and because of, this absolute Being. It is in relationship with this Being that we find ultimate meaning and purpose.

This Being is what we call God. I think he gets a kick out of our little "theories." If the world "evolved," it was God who evolved it. Man could not have evolved from anything other than man, since man was created independently of nature. God is the one who gives meaning and direction to life. Apart from Him, we have no logical reason to exist. In fact, without God nothing *could* exist. God is the ultimate self-evident fact, but we humans like to "hide the evidence" because we like thinking that we're in charge.

Even atheists believe in a higher power, though they don't use the term "God." Their god may be nature, or themselves, or their sciences; but their very desire to believe in *something* is God at work in them. No one has ever lived who has not known deep within himself that he is not his own creator. At some point, every sane person questions the meaning of his or her own existence. The person who says there is no God has never seriously questioned his own reason for being. He is like the boy whistling in the dark as he walks past the graveyard. He denies God's existence because he has no power over his own inevitable, inescapable, and very personal death. Atheism is a fairytale in which, if you can pretend there is no Creator, you can cause the Creator to simply not be. To acknowledge God would be to acknowledge reality, and in so doing, you'd have to come to terms with Him. Psalm 14:1 says, *"The fool has said in his heart, 'there is no God'."*

You may be wondering what all of this God-stuff has to do with the values of life, liberty, and property, as well as the principles of individualism, self-reliance, and personal responsibility. My firm conviction is that these values and principles are not man-made but are given to us. They are the foundation of a "natural law" that we are born into. The reason we know instinctively that slavery is wrong is because we know freedom is right. The reason we abhor death is that we know life is the ultimate value. The reason we instinctively feel violated when something we possess is taken away (even from infancy) is because we have a God-given design to interact with our world via property. Just observe a kid playing with other kids. You will inevitably hear the lament, "That's not fair!" because it is a fact of life that ownership of property is a right. **Our "property" consists of our bodies, thoughts, ideas, dreams, time, energy, personal space, and possessions, and also the things we create through the *use* of these attributes.**

The code of self-reliance calls for me to share what I know with you and then let go of the outcome of that sharing. You can take it or leave it. But I do admit that I have a stake in getting as many of my fellow Americans to understand and act on the ideas in this book. I have a child, and most of the people I know and love have children who are growing up in the world that will be shaped by the ideas and actions of others. So, my primary goal is to get as many Americans as possible to see that their votes have consequences for good or ill. They will either vote for freedom or against it based on their understanding of what freedom is.

Freedom is a God-given, natural right. But because not all people believe this, many will deny freedom to others by force. Those who understand that they have a right to freedom have to fight those who would take it away for their own purposes. Please indulge me as I explain the origin of life, liberty, and property, so that you may become one who understands this most precious gift of freedom.

We are very fortunate to have been born into a time when science has been able to not only probe deeply into outer space and show us the wonders of the universe, but also to go deep within the basic building blocks of life and find out what is there. When scientists discovered the atom, everyone thought they found the building blocks of the universe. Over time, they began breaking down an atom into its constituent parts—protons, neutrons, electrons, and the space and electrical charges between them. Scientists who study quantum physics have found that these parts of an atom really just consist of pure energy. The atom is not a real physical presence as we think of it, but rather it is the presence of that energy.

The energy that comprises an atom is what makes everything we know of as matter. In other words, nothing can even exist apart from that pure energy. Everything is energy. When you look at a rock, a desk, a bird, or even a person, they all are made of the same basic thing—*energy* expressing itself as various kinds of atoms. It's only logical and obvious that a super-intelligent, super-energy source has arranged all of the various combinations of atoms to make and sustain everything that exists. Take away that energy source, and everything would disappear.

I recently learned of the further discovery that this energy is made up of light and, in fact, *is* light.[7] That's quite a coincidence, because the Bible says that the very first thing God called into existence was light. Nothing existed when God created the world, but He had to create it out of something. So, He pulled light out of His very being. He had to have something with which to build. Where else was He going to get building materials? When you look at the first chapter of John in the Bible, you can see that this light is called *"the light of men,"*[8] but man cannot *comprehend* it. That same chapter of the book of John says, *"He is the true Light which gives light to every man who comes into the world."*

We see because of light. We think because of this light. When we understand something, we say, "Now I see!" God says, *"This is the message we have heard from him and declare to you: God is light; in him there is no darkness at all."*[9] I do not think that science will be able to get beneath the light to "discover" the Spirit that causes the light. But, as with most of quantum physics, that Spirit will be *inferred*, because the light is there. Light merely makes the unseeable seen, but you can't really *see* light itself. Psalm 104:2 says of God: "*[You] cover Yourself with light as with a garment, [You] stretch out the heavens like a curtain.*" The light of God is hidden from our sight because it is so powerful we cannot even glimpse it and live. When Moses came down from Mount Sinai after having received the Ten Commandments from God, his face shined so brightly that no one could look at him.[10] He had to wear a veil over his face to keep from blinding people.

Because the very building block of our existence is light, and God is light, then by the fact that we're created "in His image" we have the capacity to know Him. This doesn't mean that whatever you believe *about* God is true of Him, but that you can know Him through what He has already revealed. You can know everything there is to know *about* a person, for example, but you can never truly *know* the person himself. You would have to actually get into that person's skin and become that other person in order to truly *know* him or her. What God has done for us is to provide a way to get into His skin. **Through Jesus' death on our behalf, He opened a portal into His very Being. The Bible tells us that we can walk through that portal simply by believing that He did this for us.** There is nothing that we can do to open that portal,[11] and there is no other portal.[12] But Jesus did not just die, He also resurrected Himself. This resurrection was a sign, an indicator, that He had power over death itself, and that death is not an end, but a beginning.

No one has ever existed that is just like you. His infinite ability to create endless variations and forms, personalities and plans, makes each one of us an individual expression of God Himself. This is why our Founders felt very strongly about protecting the individual and giving the individual power over government. Christianity is the force that showed the world that slavery was wrong because of the inherent worth of each individual. In God's eyes, the individual is of supreme value.

When we depend on government, people, institutions, ideas, drugs, or anything else other than God to give us meaning, purpose, and sustenance, we make those things into gods. The reason God commanded *"You shall have no other gods before me"*[13] is that other gods enslave us, whether those gods be money, government, other people, or any thing we may desire or depend upon other than God. God's very nature is freedom, and because we are created in His image, we are designed to be free. He put this unquenchable desire for freedom inside each human. When we seek to enslave ourselves to government, through socialism, communism, or any other ism, we are going against our very nature as His free creations.

Limited self-government is a powerful tool in the arsenal of freedom, because it places a demand on people to own themselves—to take responsibility for their God-given lives. Our natural rights to life, liberty, and property belong to us as gifts from our Creator, and, as such, they are ours by His "natural law." Thomas Jefferson said, *"God who gave us life, gave us liberty. And can the liberties of a nation be thought secure when we have removed their only firm basis, a conviction in the minds of the people that these liberties are a gift from God?"*

In explaining natural law, property rights, and man's relation to other men, John Locke, a British philosopher of the 18th century, wrote the following in his *Second Treatise of Government*:

> *Though the earth, and all inferior creatures be common to all men, yet every man has a "property" in his own "person." This nobody has any right to but himself. The "labour" of his body and the "work" of his hands, we may say, are properly his. Whatsoever, then, he removes out of the state that Nature hath provided and left it in, he hath mixed his labour with it, and joined to it something that is his own, and thereby makes*

it his property. It being by him removed from the common state Nature placed it in, it hath by this labour something annexed to it that excludes the common right of other men. For this "labour" being the unquestionable property of the labourer, no man but he can have a right to what that is once joined to, at least where there is enough, and as good left in common for others.[14]

To have a "property" in one's person, then, is the most basic right we have. This is why the right to life is fundamental. Life is property. It seems kind of self-evident, but without life, you have nothing.

The Founding Fathers were familiar with Locke's works, and Jefferson referred to Locke in the Declaration of Independence when he said, *"We hold these truths to be self-evident, that all men are created equal, that they are endowed by their Creator with certain unalienable Rights, that among these are Life, Liberty and the pursuit of Happiness."* Locke's property right included a person's own body and mind and the fruits of the labor of one's body and mind. Thus, a person's life is his property, and his Liberty is a property. The "pursuit of happiness" refers to a person's dreams, goals, and aspirations, and the fruits of his efforts to attain those. So, *"the pursuit of happiness"* is a property belonging to man, because God made man to be a goal-seeking creature. Man, by nature, must be free to pursue his dreams. As Americans, we are blessed to have a property in our freedom.

But freedom would not be freedom if it did not also mean the freedom to do evil. So, to protect us from ourselves, we form communities and create governments for the express purpose of creating and enforcing standards of conduct. A government's purpose is to defend the individual from his neighbors' sin nature—his tendency to take property instead of working for it—and from outside invaders such as foreign armies. The Declaration says, "… *That to secure these rights, Governments are instituted among Men, deriving their just powers from the consent of the governed.…*" Locke said it this way in his Treatise:

> *If man in the state of Nature be so free as has been said, if he be absolute lord of his own person and possessions, equal to the greatest and subject to nobody, why will he part with his freedom, this empire, and subject himself to the dominion and control of any other power? To which it is obvious to answer, that though in the state of Nature he hath such a right, yet the enjoyment of it is very uncertain and constantly exposed to the invasion of others; for all being kings as much as he, every man his equal, and the greater part no strict observers of equity and justice, the enjoyment of the property he has in this state is very unsafe, very insecure. This makes him willing to quit this condition which, however free, is full of fears and continual dangers; and it is not without reason that he seeks out and is willing to join in society with others who are already united, or have a mind to unite for the mutual preservation of their lives, liberties and estates, which I call by the general name—property. The great and chief end, therefore, of men uniting into commonwealths, and putting themselves under government, is the preservation of their property; to which in the state of Nature there are many things wanting.*[15]

We give government the power to use deadly force to protect us from criminals and invaders—those who would take our lives or the fruits of our lives from us. By giving government this power, we are not giving up our lives nor our responsibility to sustain our lives. We are merely making a contract: *You, Government, protect me and my family from foreign invaders and criminals, and we'll give you the authority and the money to do that.* It's a limited contract—limited to the protection of life, liberty, and property.

Unfortunately, many people have come to believe that if we have a right to "pursue happiness" as stated in the Declaration, and the government has a duty to provide for "the general welfare," as stated in the Constitution, then it is government's duty to provide for our material happiness. Just watch next time there is a natural "disaster" such as a hurricane. People will be all over the media clamoring for government to do something, and billions of dollars will flow from the United States Treasury to the victims of the disaster, with all its attendant waste and fraud. And yet, hurricane-life happens day-in-and-day-out in America, where citizens demand that government help them in a multitude of ways. When we begin to depend on government like this, we enslave ourselves.

Any parent will tell you that there is no end to children's wants. It pains me to say it, but we have become a nation of children, looking to government as our parent-god. This is where our government's paternalism comes from. Government didn't impose it. People demanded it first; then government imposed it. Now it is an imposing machine, set on "auto-parent," spoiling and care-taking. And government has become addicted to its own false role. Defeating this ideology can only be done one way. It will be a simple but painful process. However, in the end, it will bring about freedom once again for our children and grandchildren:

1. We'll have to get some adults into Congress, the White House, and the Supreme Court who can and will say "No" to the constant demands of the people to have all their needs met by government.

2. Individuals will have to be educated to become self-reliant. This will mean returning public school curriculum to real American history.

3. Those of us who still adhere to the founding principles and values of America, as embodied in the Declaration and the Constitution,

will have to "fight" for them in a non-violent way. This fight will occur by convincing others of the moral superiority of freedom over security.

At this point, it seems that the anti-freedom forces outnumber us. But the American spirit of liberty will prevail if we do not give up. I believe that a new, more mature, stronger America will emerge from this struggle. Unfortunately, it may take a dramatic loss of freedom first, but a new appreciation for freedom will emerge from the discovery by our fellow citizens that the tyranny of statism, socialism, and communism is not the way.

We are fighting to overcome the shortfalls, and we are filling in the blank spaces, left by government-run education. Our fellow citizens should not be feared, hated, or pitied. They just need to have their education in life, liberty and property completed. The next chapter is a simple explanation of what private property is and why it should be respected and defended by individuals and government.

Chapter Four

Pretty Rocks

"The desire of gold is not for gold. It is for the means of freedom and benefit".

— Ralph Waldo Emerson

"The blessing of the Lord makes one rich, and He adds no sorrow with it."

— Proverbs 10:22

Imagine that you live back, say, in the year 553. You are walking through a forest and find a nice-looking tree limb on the ground. It is straight and strong. You figure you can make something out of it, like a spear. So you bend down and pick it up.

Few people are on the earth at that time, so you are ninety-nine percent sure that no one owns that limb, and no one owns the land where you found it. You now hold it in your hand and want to keep it. So, here's a simple question: Who owns the limb?

Before you picked it up, no one owned it. You simply saw it on the ground, and the limb was preparing to rot. Now, since you went to the effort to pick it up, you own it. By natural right, the tree limb belongs to you, and you can do anything with it you wish. You could throw it away, give it away, burn it, or sell it. So, you decide the most advantageous thing to do with it is to make a spear and then trade it for something else that you need.

You go to work, adding value to the limb by removing the bark and carving it into a beautiful spear. You make a spearhead for it from a stone that you have shaped and sharpened. You now have something of value. You found it. You own it. And by mixing your labor with it, it has become a piece of property. Remember Locke's statement from the previous chapter: *"Whatsoever, then, he removes out of the state that Nature hath provided and left it in, he hath mixed his labour with it, and joined to it something that is his own, and thereby makes it his property."*

So now, you want to trade the spear for some vegetables that your friend has grown, but you get an idea that you could leverage your spear (your property) to gain even more. So, you use the spear to kill a deer; then you have two pieces of property. You use the deer's antlers to make knife handles, and you prepare the hide so it can be made into clothing. All of it belongs to you, because you have used your time and energy to produce it.

You then take the things you made to a place where other people gather to trade what they have grown or found and made useful. Among the items being traded are vegetables, grains, meat, baskets, pottery, and animal skins. You trade your deer meat for some vegetables, and a knife handle for a basket in which to put them. You head home with your purchases. You have obtained the things you needed through the efforts of your mind and body. You have used your time well. You leveraged it to buy yourself more time.

Now that you have enough to eat for a few days, you have time to start building that cabin you want so you can ask that girl to marry you. As you walk through the forest, you carry your spear to protect yourself from predators. You feel good. You are taking care of yourself, and you feel confident that you can take care of a wife and eventually your children. You don't know it, but you are a free, self-reliant capitalist. What you *do* know is that your future is limited only by your dreams of how you will continue to leverage your time and energy.

A short two years later, you've finished your cabin, you've married the girl of your dreams, and you have a child. A second one is on the way! You have also accumulated more antlers and have even designed a new gardening tool from the antlers. Your "neighbors" have all wanted one, and you have spent a good deal of your time and energy building and improving the tool. Now word is out that you are the maker of a valuable time-saving device, and people from all around are coming to get one from you.

The problem is that they want to trade grain and vegetables, and you already have enough of those. If you take more in trade, the vegetables will rot before you can eat them. So, one of the traders offers to give you some pretty rocks in exchange for the tool. First you think he's crazy, because you have no use for pretty rocks—or any rocks for that matter. Then he says you can give the rocks back to him at his farm in the spring, and he will give you the vegetables that are in season at the time. In other words, if you take the rocks now, you can get the vegetables when you actually need them.

Wow! You think this is a great idea. The only problem is that you don't know if you can trust him or not. What if he doesn't live up to his bargain? What if he dies? What if he produces a bad crop? He tells you that his neighbor a few miles away, whom you know and trust, will also take the pretty rocks in exchange for his crops, because his neighbor can also trade them with others, who in turn, will use them to trade also for the things they need.

This all sounds crazy to you at first. Everyone trading useless pretty rocks for valuable, hard-earned items? So, you tell him you'll try it this one time, just to see how the plan will work. He gives you seven pretty rocks for one of your garden tools, and he says he'll give you the grain and vegetables you need in the spring. He goes away happy. You look after him, wondering....

This deal saves him the trouble of having to haul his grain and vegetables to the market. It saves you from having to turn away his purchase because you don't need what he has available to trade right now. Imagine what this could mean if you could do the same kind of deal with that guy over in the other valley—the guy who makes really good skinning knives in exchange for venison. He would probably appreciate not having to worry about the meat going bad if he doesn't need a whole deer when you come to trade for a knife! But the really appealing idea is that you won't have to drag that carcass across the mountains! He can just use the pretty rocks to buy the meat he needs from someone who lives on his side of the mountain.

Now, you've got to convince him that those pretty rocks are going to be valuable enough to actually trade. And the way to do that is to find the hunter over there who will be willing to take the rocks and trade them to someone who has what he wants. So, you go over the mountain with just a few pretty rocks. It's a lot easier to carry them than a whole deer!

As you trudge across the mountain, you ask questions of yourself that you've never considered before: "What if everyone traded pretty rocks for the things they needed? It would be so much easier. What if someone were to start storing up the items that most people needed, and the people could just come to one place and trade the pretty rocks for the items? Sure would save a lot of time and energy. And isn't that what all this is about? Saving time and energy? After all, everything we do, everything everyone does, takes time and energy. If we all could just do what we do best, like me making garden tools, and Joe growing tomatoes, and Frank's wife making those blankets, and so on...then we could save a lot of time and energy to be free to

Pretty Rocks

do other things. I could hire a young man to kill and skin the deer in exchange for a part of the meat, and then I would have the antlers for making garden tools. Wow, just think how many garden tools I'll have time to make if I don't have to spend my time and energy hunting. I could trade them for the pretty rocks and then hide the pretty rocks so that I will have them to buy food when we need it.

If I followed this plan, then I'd have enough free time to spend building cabins for other people, which is what I *really* like to do. And they could pay me with more pretty rocks, which I could store for the future. Who knows, maybe I could even leave the pretty rocks for my wife and children when I die. I can live with so much less stress, knowing that they would be taken care of when I'm gone, at least until the pretty rocks run out.

But wait! Why couldn't I just train the wife and children to make the garden tools or even something of more value that people need, so that they, too, will be able to trade for the pretty rocks!"

Well, it takes some time and effort, but eventually everyone for miles around begins to see the value of using the pretty rocks. It saves everyone so much time and energy that they are able to concentrate on doing what they do best. Within a few years, everyone begins to earn more pretty rocks than they actually need to meet their basic needs. Many are able to save some of their pretty rocks each time they make an exchange with someone.

Some of the people, however, spend all their pretty rocks as soon as they get them, never saving for anything. They have to work all the time to just get enough to survive, so they don't have extra that would grant them the free time to build another way of earning more pretty rocks. In this way, they stay poor. They say that everything costs too much for them to be able to save any pretty rocks. They came close to having all the nice things everyone else had, but they wasted a lot on fire-water and the tumbly-stones game. They didn't save for the future. So, when they lost pretty rocks at the games, or traded their rocks on things they really didn't need, they borrowed more pretty rocks until they owed more than they earned.

Over time, you manage to save many pretty rocks, and you are secure in knowing your family will not starve even if something might happen to you. Life is good. From the finding of a tree limb in the forest, to the building of a small business, you have built a secure life for yourself and your family. You even have enough to help your friends when they need it, and you are happy too. You give some of your pretty rocks to young mothers with children whose fathers have died, and you give to old widows with no one to provide for them. You feel rich, because you are able to help them.

Then one day, some men from a neighboring valley come and tell you that they have formed a council to oversee the trade in the area, because it seems that some people are accumulating more pretty rocks than others. They have come up with a plan to take some pretty rocks from everyone to give to others who do not have as many.

At first, you think it is a practical joke, but these dudes look serious, and they have servants with spears behind them. So you ask who those others are who don't have as many pretty rocks as everyone else, and they give you a few names. You start to laugh, because you know some of them. They're the ones who have traded plenty, even competing against you in the cabin-building business, and they have had many pretty rocks pass through their hands. But they wasted them on things they didn't need, like fire-water and games of chance, and all sorts of things that do not save any time and energy.

You look the strange men square in the eye and say, "No," you're not going to give any of your pretty rocks to those people, because you are already giving to others who have truly worked hard and have not squandered their income, and who have legitimate needs.

The men tell you that everyone must give to the fund so that everyone else will have just as many pretty rocks. You have no choice in the matter. You tell them you've never heard of such a thing and that they have no business on your property and should leave now. But their servants with spears step up and point their weapons at you.

Then the thief-dudes start looking around your cabin, turning furniture over, looking inside and under your belongings, and they aren't careful about it. You know they won't find the pretty rocks, because you've hidden them in the woods where no one knows but you and your wife. The back of your neck and head get very hot, and your heart starts to pound. You're not thinking clearly, but you sense that these men are up to no good. You have worked long and hard for many years, putting your time and energy into the savings you have. If you were to give them even one pretty rock, you could not live with yourself because of the shame and humiliation for allowing these bullies to take part of your life away. You're angrier than you've ever been, and you've had enough!

Just then, your wife comes in the door to the cabin, and the thief-dudes gruffly demand that she tell them where the pretty rocks are. They have no business talking to your wife, so you lunge at them. You manage to get one of them by the arm and twist it as you push him to the door. As you do, you feel a stabbing pain in your side. You've been speared. Your hot anger flares even more, and you push the man outside to the ground as you bleed. You turn to get the other man, but you must first deal with the spearmen.

You reach for your own trusted spear, the one that started you in business. As you grab it and start to turn, you feel something tear through your back and out through your chest. You realize you're going to die. As you breathe your last breath, you pray that God will protect your wife and children and that she will not tell the thief-dudes where the pretty rocks are. They may be able to take your life, but they'll not be able to take the time and energy you put into making your family financially secure. Or will they?

Money is a limited resource, because money is a representation of our time and energy. Our time and energy are really the only things we have to spend in this short life. Each human has a "property" in their time and energy. When we earn money, we are actually just trading the limited resource of our lives for pieces of paper, or digits on a computer screen. We use money to trade portions of our lives for portions of the lives of other people. We only have so much capacity for labor because of our physical and mental limitations. These limitations make our time and energy scarce resources, and because they are scarce, they have value.

Money has no value in itself. It is just a tool for convenience, just a form of exchange. If you were all alone in the world and had a pile of gold a mile high and a mile square, you'd have nothing of value. Money only has the value that people agree to place on it, based on varying degrees of scarcity, effort, and need. If we *trust* that we can spend the money for things we need and want, and we *trust* that other people will have the same *trust* in the money and its value, then we can use it. Trust is essential to the value of money.

Prices are set based on the value we assign to time and energy. The more we value a person's time and energy, the more we will be willing to pay for his or her services and/or products. If someone makes something that will save us time and energy, then we value that product highly, because we will be able to use the saved time and energy on some other activity that we value more highly. All trade is simply exchanging something that we value for something that we value **more** at the time of the exchange.

For example, I value the fifty bucks I earned by using my time and energy to paint a door for someone who chose to use his time and energy to do something he valued more highly than his fifty bucks. But my stomach values food more highly than the fifty bucks, so I exchange that 50 dollars at the grocery store, knowing that the food

I buy will bring value to my life and the lives of my family members. Then I will be able to take the energy generated by that food and do more work to earn more money. The grocer will be able to exchange the 50 dollars to buy more groceries to sell and to pay his employees, who are trading their time and energy for the money they will be paid. The trading goes on and on, day-in-and-day-out, all over the world.

So, how is it that I can only get fifty bucks for the two hours of my time to paint a door for a man who is a doctor, while in that same amount of time the doctor earns two hundred bucks at *his* job?

The key to income is demand. For example, a doctor may earn two-hundred thousand dollars in one year of time, while I may only make fifty-thousand dollars a year as a painter. This is because the services the doctor provides are **more scarce** than the services the painter provides. In other words, there are plenty of painters out there, and they all are competing for available jobs, so the people who hire painters know they can always find someone else to do the job. The supply of painters is high, while the demand for them is comparatively low.

Also, doctors spend many years in college and in training, and the extensive scientific study they go through is grueling. They have to pass tests and get licensed; they must pay outrageous insurance premiums just for the privilege of working 80 hours a week or more. Most people couldn't do it. Most people wouldn't to do it! Doctors get paid for their knowledge and skill, not necessarily their time, so the comparison to house painting is not an accurate reflection of the time and energy idea. However in the United States, where we have a mostly free market in medicine (for now) there is financial incentive for people to become doctors, although you have to have more than a desire for money to become a doctor.

If the profit were removed, for example, if government were to "socialize" health care by telling doctors what they will be paid and how they will practice, the supply of doctors would become smaller and smaller because fewer people would choose to exchange their time and energy for a huge debt and a life of 80 hour weeks with little payoff in the end. However, the demand would remain high because everyone needs health care. Most people can do their own house painting if they have to, but not many people can do their own surgery!

So, what happens when the supply is not enough to meet the demand? Prices go up to make it worthwhile to meet the demand. But if prices are regulated by government, two things would happen: Doctors pay would go down as their patient load goes up to meet the demand. In such a case, most doctors would find somewhere else to go to practice medicine, or they would choose another profession altogether, which would further decrease the supply of doctors, which would further increase costs for health care. Then, government would have to import doctors from other countries who would, for a while, accept the government mandated limits on what they can charge. Eventually the imported doctors would find the pay not to be worth the stress, and they would move to where they could get paid what they are worth, or get out of the business altogether.

Let's now consider something that is neither necessary nor essential, like entertainment. Look at a football, basketball, or baseball player who gets millions of dollars per year for playing a game! The only value he offers is temporary entertainment. When a game is over, nothing of monetary value is taken away by the people who watched. In fact, if there were no football, basketball, or baseball games for people to watch, maybe they'd get out and exercise, study, or build more. Games are of little value, but many people like the entertainment value they receive from watching them. Since so many people are willing to pay for tickets to watch someone else play a game, and television stations are willing to pay huge amounts of money for advertising during the airing of those games, lots of money is available to pay huge salaries to those who play the games well.

The supply of people who play games well is fairly small compared to the supply of people who can sit in an easy chair and eat junk food while watching them. The players earn those huge salaries because they have skills and abilities most people don't have but are willing to pay to see. Nothing about this is unfair. It is the free market. If you think it's unfair, maybe you should try out for the NBA. You would quickly see that the players are not getting paid for their time, but for the talent they display.

The same is true for actors and actresses. The only thing they have to do is pretend to be someone else in a convincing and entertaining way. Not exactly hard work, but not many people can do it well. Since millions of people are willing to pay to watch them do what they do, they get the big bucks. Again, nothing about this is unfair. It's the free market. Never envy someone else's income. They are only doing what you would probably do if you had the same desire, talent, training, and opportunity!

Next time you find yourself complaining about how much money someone else makes compared to yourself, just ask yourself how much effort you have put into educating or training yourself to make yourself more valuable to others. It's the value that you provide to the marketplace that determines your financial worth. (Don't get this confused with spiritual or personal worth.) Your financial worth is the amount of money you can earn based on the value of your skills or talents to the free market. **The free market is simply the whole arena of people trading their time and energy with each other.**

This whole process of free markets and the trading of time and energy is just the natural order of the world. A tree exchanges oxygen for carbon dioxide. A fire exchanges heat for oxygen. Atoms exchange electrons to become other atoms. Plants collect light to make chlorophyll, which nourishes animals, which become food for other animals and man, and so on. Everything in nature is constantly exchanging. So the free exchange of time and energy between people is the God-designed, natural order. Conflicts erupt when this order is upset.

When people spend a lot of time and energy learning a skill, developing a talent, or just saving money they've earned by long, hard work, they do not like it when someone comes along and demands that they give a portion of it away. We don't mind giving of our own volition, and we freely give in response to God's desire that we help the poor, but no one likes being robbed. No one likes having a portion of his time and energy taken from him either by manipulation, inflation, or by force.

Let's say that you earn sixty thousand dollars a year as a salesman. Over a period of several years, you managed to save thirty thousand dollars to buy a certain car that you have always wanted. So, you buy the car and you drive it with pride. You put your time and energy into owning that car. That car represents six months of your life, because it cost you a half-year's salary to buy it. (For this example, let's ignore the income tax you paid on your salary and the sales tax you paid on the car.)

One night, as you sleep, a thief comes and steals your car. You wake up the next morning and find it gone. You are very upset. Why? Are you upset because you have to find another way to get to work today? Probably. But you are really upset, and you feel violated, because the thief not only took that hunk of steel and vinyl. He took half a year of your life. You would not be upset if you had given that thirty thousand dollars to a charity that you believed in, because you will have made the free choice to do so.

When we use our time and energy to attain property legally, it is rightfully ours to do with what we choose. When someone, including government, takes that property, it is taking our time and energy, our very lives. **This is why we had no income tax for the first hundred and thirty seven years of our existence as a nation.** Our Founders, and most citizens, would not have stood for it because it would have been immoral and unconstitutional.

In a later chapter we'll get into the moral alternative to the income tax, and the benefits of making free choices. But first, lets find out what happens when the element of choice is removed and government "legally" takes from some, according to their means, and gives to others, according to their needs.[1]

Chapter Five

What's Wrong With Socialism?

"America will never be destroyed from the outside. If we falter and lose our freedoms, it will be because we destroyed ourselves."

— Abraham Lincoln

"He who is surety for a stranger will suffer, but one who hates surety is secure."

— Proverbs 11:15

When people have the incentive to work and the freedom to do the work they enjoy, many good things happen. Needs are met, and desires are fulfilled. Nowhere in the world has this been more abundantly displayed than in America. Free trade, free thought, and free expression of ideas are the means by which the world has been blessed by Americans. **When individuals are allowed to prosper by the unlimited imagination and ingenuity**

God gave them, everyone benefits. For examples, you need look no further than the cotton gin, the internal combustion engine, the jet, the personal computer, and a million other inventions that sprang up from the fertile ground of freedom. None of these would have been possible if the inventors did not have the freedom to invent, with financial rewards as incentive. But incentive declines in proportion to taxation, regulation, and control by government.

The preamble to the Constitution reads as follows:

> *We the People of the United States, in Order to form a more perfect Union, establish Justice, insure domestic Tranquility, provide for the common defence, promote the general Welfare, and secure the Blessings of Liberty to ourselves and our Posterity, do ordain and establish this Constitution for the United States of America.*

The four little words that seem to have caused the socialism-creep we have seen over the last hundred years are, *"promote the general welfare."* Well-meaning people have interpreted this phrase to mean that whatever government can do to make life better for all, it should do. It is a wide-flung net that has caught many otherwise free citizens in the trap of expecting government to make life better for them.

The actual intent of the phrase, "promote the general welfare," is to spread *freedom of opportunity* as wide and as deep as possible. When the Founders penned, "…and to promote the general welfare," it was to acknowledge the legitimate role of government as a protector against foreign and domestic enemies, so that all citizens could be free to pursue their own dreams. It meant protecting inventors and entrepreneurs from having their intellectual property diminished by thieves. It meant protecting farmers' lands and staying out of the way of free enterprise. Our Founders understood free market capitalism to be the only way by which men and women could exercise their inborn desire to excel. So, when the Founders thought of "general welfare," they had in mind "free markets and limited interference." The term "general welfare" did *not* mean what we think of as government welfare today. The "general" welfare meant the common good of all, not any particular group. It did not mean redistribution of income, but equal protection of all citizens under the law.

During the recent Presidential campaign, I heard candidate Obama say, *"the American people want government to solve their problems."* The fact that he won the election with the votes of millions with similar beliefs was a clear turning point in American history. They thought they were making history because of skin color, but the history that has emerged is one of more government dependence for the many, higher tax rates for the few, and government takeovers of once-private industries, leading to diminished incentive for job creation.

Already now, half of our fellow citizens are working as hard as they can to support their families and to stay ahead of rising taxes, while the other half are working as hard as they can to get control of that tax money by way of government. Some are doing it on purpose. I suspect that most people are doing it without even knowing what they're doing, such as the young lady I saw rejoicing because, now that she has the president of her choice, she won't have to make her car or house payments or worry about putting gas in her car! Indeed, a large segment of the United States population not only believes it is government's job to relieve them of their financial responsibilities and provide for their every need, but they also think of government as an enabling parent, ready to jump to the rescue whenever any personal pain is looming.

The assumption that government should provide anything other than protection from criminals and invading armies has to stop—and soon—or we will never be able to climb out of the multi-trillion dollar hole we've gotten ourselves into!

Have you ever wondered how it is that an immigrant from another country, with no money, speaking little or no English, and knowing no one, can come to this country and within a few years be very wealthy? Yet, millions of us born in this land of opportunity complain and moan about how the odds are stacked against us by class, race, location, physical appearance, red tape, lack of "funding," and so on. What does the immigrant have that we don't? **I strongly believe he has a greater appreciation for freedom and does not expect anyone else to give him anything.**

Many who are born into this freedom tend to take it for granted and end up wasting opportunities to improve themselves and their financial situations. It is extremely sad to see our fellow citizens looking to government to "solve their problems." Government dependence, even to a small degree, robs people of their dignity, their incentive, and their God-given purpose. In the end, dependence on government is what kills freedom. As long as you are dependent on anyone, you are not free.

Webster's dictionary defines freedom as *"exemption or liberation from the control of some other person or some arbitrary power."* John Quincy Adams said, *"Posterity: you will never know how much it has cost my generation to preserve your freedom. I hope you will make good use of it."* One of the main goals of this book is to re-awaken that sense of gratitude within Americans for the great gift we have been given at such a great cost to so many.

World history shows plenty of people who have been more than willing to tell you how to run your life. People have owned, controlled, and manipulated other people from the beginning of human existence. We have no less a problem with that today than at any time in the past. It's just more sophisticated today. In fact, manipulation by so-called "leaders" has become an art form, and the manipulation is so slick that many don't even know it's happening until it's too late.

The fact that so many support progressive and socialist policies today is an indication of the shortfalls of government schools.

Ignorance of simple economic and historical facts are the true cost of allowing government to have a monopoly on education. I just recently heard of a survey of Americans in which only fifty-three percent of adults think capitalism is the correct way to organize an economy. People who advocate socialism are never the ones who have lived under it, and they are rarely the ones paying the taxes. It's always the disgruntled who want others to take care of them. They have no idea they are forging the chains of their own slavery. Samuel Adams wrote, *"If Virtue & Knowledge are diffused among the People, they will never be enslav'd. This will be their great Security."*

Socialism is defined not only by the collection of taxes from income. Socialism is also the taking of private property to "save the planet," to "protect endangered species," or to sell to another private citizen for development, which will bring in greater property taxes for government. Socialism is also governmental control of industries like banks, auto companies, insurance companies, and the like.

Socialism is the means by which any government takes power from individuals by promising some perceived good, such as housing, health care, retirement, etc. It vests power in the government, or rather, in a few individuals at the head of government who are not subject to their own edicts and would never subject their own families to the limitations of their ideas.

Webster's New Collegiate Dictionary defines socialism as:

> *1. theory or system of social organization that advocates the vesting of the ownership and control of the means of production and distribution, of capital, land, etc., in the community as a whole [under socialism, "community" means government].*
>
> *2. procedure or practice in accordance with this theory.*
>
> *3. (in Marxist theory) the stage following capitalism in the transition of a society to communism, characterized by the imperfect implementation of collectivist principles.*

What's Wrong With Socialism?

If that last one didn't grip your heart with fear, you may be part of the problem. Communism was responsible for the death of hundreds of millions of people throughout the world in the twentieth century. Just ask some Jews, Russians, Chinese, Vietnamese, Cambodians, Cubans, and the list goes on. Anyone who advocates communism as a good idea in the twenty-first century is in need of some serious therapy.

Socialism is a *"stage following capitalism in transition to communism."* Hmm. I wonder why our current Congress seems so bent on socializing the banks, the auto makers, the mortgage industry, health care, etc? Could it be that they, too, have been corrupted by mis-education into believing that only big government can solve problems? Or maybe they are just smarter than the rest of us. The great economist, Thomas Sowell, said, *"Socialism in general has a record of failure so blatant that only an intellectual could ignore or evade it."*

One of the great tragedies of the twentieth century in America was the dumbing down of education, especially concerning history and religion. Whether it was done deliberately or not, I'll leave to the intellectuals to debate, but you can readily see that many government school textbooks don't even begin to tell the true history of our founding. My point here is that the appreciation for the sacrifices made for our freedom, and the understanding of the foundation of freedom, has gone the way of the plow horse and the musket. We have come to think we have better ways now. We do not realize that we are all standing on the shoulders of patriots and prophets. Lack of appreciation for freedom has laid the foundation for extremely dangerous political policies that threaten our hard-won liberty. Thomas Jefferson said in 1807, *"History, in general, only informs us what bad government is."* **The history that warns us against socialism is recent and bloody, and the fact that a majority of Americans seem to have no problem with it now is both baffling** and frightening.

Economist Henry Hazlitt has rightly noted that, *"The ideas which now pass for brilliant innovations and advances are in fact mere revivals of ancient errors, and a further proof of the dictum that those who are ignorant of the past are condemned to repeat it."* Since those currently in power in the United States, and the majority that put them there, were not taught the true history of the Soviet Union, China, and the socialized nations of western Europe, they are taking all of us down the same pot-holed road of centralized planning and government control.

I don't put all the blame on the current administration. As I said, this assault on freedom has been going on for many years at all levels of government. **Through the courts, the legislature, and the executive branch, private property rights have been eroding so gradually but surely that we are like the proverbial frog that has been boiled.** I hope to show that although socialism promises to bring security to the many, in reality it enslaves us all. Thomas Jefferson said, *"Dependence begets subservience and venality, suffocates the germ of virtue, and prepares fit tools for the designs of ambition."*

When government begins taking more responsibility, more authority, and more money than is necessary for the protection of our natural rights, it ceases to become a good servant and commences to be an evil master. We have allowed government to do what we would never do ourselves. God said, **"You shall not covet your neighbor's house. You shall not covet your neighbor's wife, or his manservant or maidservant, his ox or donkey, or anything that belongs to your neighbor."** We can easily see that when we take something that belongs to someone else, it is wrong; but when we give government the power to do the same thing, it somehow seems okay. But it is not okay.

To "covet" is "to desire wrongfully, inordinately, or without due regard for the rights of others: to covet another's property." In other words, socialism is envy in action. Winston Churchill said, *"Socialism is a philosophy of failure, the creed of ignorance, and the gospel of envy, its inherent virtue is the equal sharing of misery."*

So, how did we get from the common belief that we were endowed by God with the rights to "life, liberty, and the pursuit of happiness" all the way to government dependence? And now, how do we step back from the precipice of ruin and get back on the path of self-reliance?

I believe the answer to the first question lies in words spoken by our recently elected President, At the National Day of Prayer breakfast in January of 2009, the President gave a speech in which he told the gathering of religious leaders how he had become a "Christian." He said that it was when he moved to Chicago and began attending a church where he saw the people reaching out to the poor and needy. (You may have heard some of the virulence that came from the pastor of that church on the national news.) It seems that the social gospel of helping the needy was being done in a spirit of resentment that there were so many people who were in need. The President had correctly interpreted the Scriptures to mean that a Christian should reach out to help others. But he incorrectly overlapped it with his understanding of Marxism, thereby coming to the conclusion that government's job is to *cause* compassionate actions to happen via redistribution of private property. I'm not criticizing Mr. Obama. **It's quite obvious that many people hold the mistaken belief that, by getting government to meet all the needs of the poor by redistributing societal wealth, they are doing "the Lord's work."** They are sincere in their beliefs although the beliefs are misguided.

Further insight into the social gospel mindset came during another speech the same year at Wesleyan University, where the President said, *"Our individual salvation depends on collective salvation."* These words revealed exactly how so many people have come to cling to government as a savior and as the only source of security. **Where**

God is replaced by man, people get emotionally attached to those men who promise "salvation" in the form of egalitarianism. Thus, government has taken the place of God for many Americans.

To be fair, his predecessor, President Bush, made a similar mistake by invoking what he called, "compassionate conservatism." Both of them have/had good intentions, but their premises are flawed. **Compassion is not government's job—it's the individual's job. Salvation is not man's job. It belongs solely to God.**

Since I can't read the mind of either President, I can only surmise from their respective statements that they assume government should legislate compassion. This social gospel mindset comes from a narrow interpretation of the New Testament, where Jesus tells people many times that they should serve the poor.[1]

Of course we should help the poor, visit the sick, clothe the naked, visit prisoners, etc. Of course we should love our neighbors as ourselves and do all of the things Jesus taught. But Jesus was speaking to people as ***individuals***. As God, Jesus knew that He had created man in His image. He had made man a free, creative agent, responsible not only to provide for himself and his family, but to help others out of his own free will. Jesus knew that for love to truly be love, it has to be voluntarily *chosen*—not forced.

Jesus did not come to change governments, but individuals. To seek to apply the gospel to governments is to create an anti-individual, anti-freedom "gospel," which is the opposite of God's will for mankind. **Jesus' mission was not to promote the redistribution of private property. He came to die for the sin of all *individuals* so that those who will humbly receive that gift can have eternal life.**[2] Serving the poor is a natural response to having received salvation through Christ's sacrifice on our behalf. It is born of gratitude, love, and compassion. But, when governments try to force people to "love their neighbor" it negates the whole point of love, which can only come from free choice. The worst part of the social gospel is that it obscures the real gospel, which provides eternal life in joy, as opposed to an eternity in total hopelessness and despair.

Proverbs 26:12 says, *"Do you see a man who is wise in his own eyes? There is more hope for a fool than for him."* A look at the mass graves all over Europe, or the piles of human skulls in Cambodia, or the concentration camps of Germany will verify that humans will almost always screw things up and cause immense suffering when not following the common sense set forth in God's Word. The social gospel serves mainly to obscure the core of the Gospel of Jesus Christ. Christ came to do for God's creations what we could not do for ourselves, that is, to reconcile us to God.[3]

It is natural for us to think that the way to eternal life in heaven is to simply do more good than bad: Just be sure your good actions outweigh your bad actions and you're home free when you stand before God on judgment day. There are a few problems with that "gospel." First, we can never know if we have actually done more good than bad, nor can we know if the "good" we have done is good enough. We have no assurance that God will see it the same way we would want Him to. Second, there is no one who *can* do more good than bad.[4] And third, by trying to justify ourselves, we ignore the gift that God has given us, that is, that he has provided through Christ alone.[5] All we need do is receive the gift God has provided. This humble acceptance is what pleases God — not any works that we may do in our own power. So, we should not help others out of a sense of trying to do the right thing. **But we do the right thing,** *as individuals,* **out of the love that He gives us in our reconciliation and oneness through Christ.**

Socialists, progressives, communists not only pervert the gospel in this way, but they pervert it further by not even taking it personally. They seek to do their good by forcing others to support their dubious causes. I'd bet a trillion bucks that if you were to check the bank accounts of redistributionists you would find very little of their own money going to ministries or other private efforts to help the poor. **The defining element of socialism is that adherents want to give away *everyone else's* money.**

The misapplication of God's commands to help the needy has caused immense suffering all around the world ever since the communist philosopher, Karl Marx, made the same unfortunate juxtaposition around 1850. I'm not saying that people who believe in a social gospel, or any other sort of "social" theory, *intend* to kill millions of people, but it has always ended up that way. Whenever you attempt to take people's hard-earned property by force, violence and death always ensue. By misapplying the Scripture's admonition to help the "poor," redistributionists have always caused more poverty, pain, and suffering. I don't know who said it originally, but it's true that *"The road to hell is paved with good intentions."*

By the way, that same politician who says that you want government to "solve your problems" also tells you not to worry, because he's only going to raise taxes on the top five percent of earners and businesses to do that. And many foolish people applaud. What do they care? It's not going to affect them. Only the "evil" rich will pay.

Three problems coincide with this attitude:

1. You can be sure that everyone will pay the higher taxes in one form or another. People who are considered to be rich invest their money in businesses that create jobs. They also are the ones who buy products you make or the service you provide. They own companies that hire people to make products to sell. When you tax the "rich," you are only causing less investment in job-creating businesses, less purchasing of whatever product or service you are employed to provide, and higher prices on everything you buy. Saying you're only going to tax the rich is like saying you're only going to dip some water out of one side of a bucket. *Everyone* suffers when *anyone's* taxes are raised.

2. The dirty little secret that socialists/progressives don't want

anyone to understand is that businesses don't pay taxes. They add the cost of taxes into their products or services and simply charge prices that pass along those taxes to the customers. **It is always only individuals who pay taxes, either directly or indirectly through price hikes.**

3. Price increases only work to a point. The free market may not allow for such an increase in price because of competition from businesses that aren't subject to the tax, such as ones located in other countries. In this case the business has to cut its costs by either cutting down on work hours or laying off employees. We cannot complain about jobs "going overseas" when we allow government to increase taxes. It's only common sense that businesses would want to produce goods at the lowest cost so that they can price their products to sell. So they go where taxes are lower, or non-existent, and labor is cheaper. A remedy for this is coming up, so keep reading.

When government takes money out of the pockets of citizens, the money is not invested in things that grow the economy. It is merely redistributed. Government redistribution programs are a dead-end game. Government takes the seeds of prosperity that would have been sown to producers, and gives them to non-producers who just eat them. **If you know anything about farming, you never want to eat your seeds. If you eat all your seeds, pretty soon you won't have any crops.** This is why communism and socialism have failed wherever they have been tried. That, and the fact that people get tired of being treated as children.

Only one sector of the economy does not suffer when taxes go up. You guessed it—government. Even when revenue goes down because of the tax increase, they simply print the money to continue their bureaucracies. Everyone in government still gets paid. They get regular increases despite performance. They are never laid off. They are even unionized! Government never suffers the consequences of its own mistakes. In fact, when a government program is shown to have failed, it just gets more money in the next budget.

This is unlikely to ever change unless we can elect enough brave statesmen and women to decrease the number of government employees and increase the ethical education of those who remain. Everyone who works for us should remember who they work for, and they should treat their fellow citizens, who pay their salaries, with respect and integrity.

It's supremely ironic that the former President of Russia, who used to run the KGB (Soviet Secret Police) in the former Soviet Union, and is currently the Prime Minister, recently warned the United States against going the way of socialism/communism. In a speech on February 20, 2009 at the World Economic Forum in Davos, Switzerland, Vladamir Putin said the United States should take a lesson from the pages of Russian history and not exercise *"excessive intervention in economic activity and blind faith in the state's omnipotence."*

"In the twentieth century, the Soviet Union made the state's role absolute," Putin said during a speech at the opening ceremony of the forum. *"In the long run, this made the Soviet economy totally uncompetitive. This lesson cost us dearly. I am sure nobody wants to see it repeated.*

"Nor should we turn a blind eye to the fact that the spirit of free enterprise, including the principle of personal responsibility of businesspeople, investors, and shareholders for their decisions, is being eroded in the last few months. **There is no reason to believe that we can achieve better results by shifting responsibility onto the state.***"*[6] (Emphasis mine.)

I never thought I'd be quoting a KGB guy to support an argument against socialism. Has the world been turned upside down or what? Clearly, there has been an erosion of the American character, will, and self-reliance. Whether it was deliberate or accidental does not matter at this point. What matters is that we now have the immense job of turning it around. We must remind people of our heritage and our responsibility to the future of mankind.

The problem is that a large number of Americans are either asleep, too busy, ignorant, or apathetic. I believe all of these play a role. The asleep have simply not been paying attention to what is going on over the past 20 years. The busy have just been trying to stay ahead of rising taxes and costs of living, and they have either been pursuing their dreams or just trying to survive. The ignorant have been actively pursuing redistributionist policies and candidates to carry them out. And the apathetic are the blissfully ignorant, seemingly unaware that a socialist tidal wave is approaching.

If America cannot turn back the march to socialism, could there ever be another beacon of freedom in the world? A century and a half ago, Abraham Lincoln said, *"My dream is of a place and a time where America will once again be seen as the last best hope of earth."* Has our time passed? Is anyone left who will fight for liberty from the socialist tide that seems to be engulfing us? Very few seem to be aware of the dangers of socialism.

Beyond the terrible consequences to the nation as a whole, just what does socialism mean for you, the individual? Let's look at the first definition of socialism we outlined earlier: Socialism is a *"system of social organization that advocates the vesting of the ownership and control of the means of production and distribution, of capital, land, etc., in the community as a whole."*

Beyond the obvious vesting of ownership in the government, such as is occurring with the bailouts of banks and other lending institutions, health care, social security, etc., there is the ownership and control of individuals through various means. We have to get past the academic understanding of the "means of production and control" in order to understand what is already happening to us and how we have steadily been giving up our self-ownership to big government.

In the previous chapter, we saw that our very first and most basic property right is the fact that we own our own lives. The property that we produce with the labor of our bodies and minds belongs to us also. We have the right to sell our property or give it away, as we see fit. A tax on the fruits of our labor is nothing less than the confiscation of our lives and our property. Earlier we saw that socialism is control of the "means of production." Our time, our energy, and therefore our money *are* our means of production. When any of these are confiscated by government, or eaten away by inflation, our means of production is diminished.

The government not only confiscates a portion of our income through taxation. In reality, government actually controls everything we earn, because *it* decides how much of it to take from us, or rather, how much we are allowed to keep. This may seem far-fetched, but think about it during the weeks leading up to April 15th each year as you jump through all the hoops government requires of you in order to "comply" with their tax policies. Government not only controls the amount of money you are allowed to keep, but it also controls your time, which is your life, as you "comply" with their mandated deadline. The Internal Revenue Service (IRS) estimates that it costs Americans no less than three-hundred and fifty billion dollars to "comply" with the income tax code each year! Talk about an unfunded mandate!

Another way that we are enslaved by socialism is the accumulation of debt. As I said in the introduction to this book, our national debt is now eleven trillion dollars! All this money is being borrowed to finance the lifestyles of people who made poor decisions and the innocent victims of those poor decisions. I believe it was Margaret Thatcher, the former Prime Minister of Great Britain, who said, *"The problem with socialism is that sooner or later you run out of other people's money."* Well, in America, we just print more!

Some may call it "spreading the wealth around," but when you have to borrow, you're not wealthy. When you are in debt, you are in poverty. When you're spending borrowed money, you're <u>spreading poverty</u> to future generations who will have to pay for it. Thomas Jefferson said, *"But with respect to future debt; would it not be wise and just for that nation to declare in the constitution they are forming that neither the legislature, nor the nation itself can validly contract more debt, than they may pay within their own age, or within the term of 19 years."*

If you were to figure in the amount owed for medical care for veterans, social security and medicare promises, Federal employee retirements, and the total interest that will be paid on that debt over the next thirty years, the total liabilities of the United States as of March 2009 are 55 trillion dollars! That's more than the gross domestic product of every nation in the world today. The people who are incurring this debt will not be around to help pay it off. It will be left to your children, their children, and probably their grand- and great grandchildren (if anyone will be able to afford having children by then).

Besides what we owe to China and other nations who have loaned us money, we owe ourselves in terms of future monetary value. When our government ran out of other people's money in 2008, we just cranked up the printing presses. This is called "monetizing the debt"—a fancy way of saying that we're broke, so we're just going to write bad checks until we get caught. Printing pieces of paper with important people's pictures on them does nothing to increase the value of money. In fact, the more paper dollars are printed, the less each dollar is worth.

The paper we carry or the digits on our computer screens are worth only what the market says they're worth. When the Federal Reserve prints large sums of money (because no one will loan us as much as we need), it increases the supply of money so that the number of dollars required to buy something goes up. This is called inflation, and it hurts us all by making the hard-earned dollars we put away today worth less and less in the future.

Your body, your mind, and your creations are the means of producing what you need to survive. Every individual has the responsibility to use those "means of production" to sustain him/herself and to support his/her family. When government controls the "means of production" through taxation, law, confiscation, and redistribution, you are not free—you do not really own your own life. When inflation makes each dollar worth less and less, the value of your labor is worth less. This is another form of government theft.

Of course, we need *some* government. But, as Thomas Jefferson said, *"that government is best which governs least."* A big government is a socialist government by definition. The bigger the government, the more money it needs to take from individuals to fund it. The more money it takes, the more it degrades the individual by controlling what he can earn, how much he can keep of what he earns, and who gets the fruits of his labor. The inability to control the fruits of our own labor is the definition of slavery. Abraham Lincoln said, *"Slavery is founded on the selfishness of man's nature—opposition to it on his love of justice. These principles are in eternal antagonism; and when brought into collision so fiercely as slavery extension brings them, shocks and throes and convulsions must ceaselessly follow."*

Our Founders had the wisdom to warn us of the Proverb that ***"The borrower is slave to the lender."***[7] They warned that debt is the chain that enslaves people. You can see it in your personal life. If you have borrowed money, that portion of your income that you must pay toward the debt each month is not yours. What most people fail to see is that the time and energy they have to put forth to earn the money to pay that debt is what constitutes their lives.

What government has done is to "socialize" the failure by spreading out the cost of their poor management to everyone now living and those yet to be born. A just and moral people would have already fired, fined, and/or arrested the House Banking Committee members that were responsible for oversight of Fannie Mae and Freddie Mac. An awake citizenry would have demanded that everyone responsible for the financial mess be replaced. But, alas, we are sleeping while the thieves are at work!

Prior generations focused on how they could leave a better world for the next generations. Responsible adults would never purposefully leave debt for their children, or anyone else, to pay off. In a letter to a friend in 1816, Thomas Jefferson told him, *"**We must not let our rulers load us with perpetual debt.**"* We have allowed this, and there is no way out but to remove those in power and devise a way of paying off the debt as soon as possible. Barriers must also be created for future leaders, to keep them from doing this again.

I believe we can solve the tax and debt problems and prevent the politicians from ever dragging us into this dilemma again. But it won't be easy. Our task is to wake up and educate enough self-reliant citizens to vote liberty in and socialism out. But first we must find out what would cause free people to exchange liberty for slavery. Once we understand that, we will know how to educate them.

Chapter Six

Parallel Nations

"The class of citizens who provide at once their own food and their own raiment, may be viewed as the most truly independent and happy."

— James Madison

"A wise and frugal government, which shall leave men free to regulate their own pursuits of industry and improvement, and shall not take from the mouth of labor and bread it has earned— this is the sum of good government."

— Thomas Jefferson

You may have heard that we are a divided nation: blue states vs. red states; black vs. white; rich vs. poor; conservatives vs. liberals; haves vs. have nots. I could go on and on with the ways we think of the divisions that exist in our nation, because there are many. However, the reality is that we are two separate nations, parallel nations, existing side by side, with completely differing world-views and values. This is why most national elections are so close to the fifty-fifty split. These parallel nations will always be polarized. It's just the nature of the beast.

One parallel nation is made up of self-reliant individuals who would never willingly give up sovereignty over their own lives to any government. They have the basic mindset that life is meant to be a challenge and an adventure—grist for the mill—so that each individual can become all that he or she can be. They view the Constitution in the light of the Founders' original intent. They continue to work to get ahead, even though government takes a larger and larger portion of the fruits of their labor each year. For lack of a better term, I'll call this self-reliant side of the nation the "parent nation," since it derives from the same ethos as the Founders. The citizens of the parent nation are rich and poor, black and white, Hispanic and Asian, sick and healthy, north and south, east and west. The citizens of the parent nation hold us together. They go to work, pay their taxes, raise their families, and live their lives as if they are responsible for their own life circumstances.

The other nation consists of those who have yet to learn self-reliance. They see themselves as victims of their life circumstances. They cling to government for security, and many even get into government positions to perpetuate their safety and security. They find the concepts of limited government, self-reliance, and individualism to be too scary. They see the Constitution as malleable and subject to modern-day needs and biases. Misleading politicians use this sort of citizen to gain power by offering more security via government. I call this the dependent nation, because they could not exist without the parent nation and the foundation lain by the Founders. **The citizens of the dependent nation are not "bad" or "wrong." They're merely fearful.**

Socialists/progressives see the world as static, set, and limited. They think that the limited amount of resources, for example, food, water, money, shelter, energy, etc., are dwindling according to population growth. They believe that in order for one person to have something, someone else must go without. In a logical sense this could be true about material things.

However, we don't live in a static world. We live in a creative, dynamic, ever-changing world. Resources may dry up in one area, but appear in abundance in another. In recent years, for example, oil and coal deposits have been discovered in North America that dwarf the deposits in the Middle East. **In an intelligently designed world, resources will always be there for the resourceful.** Were poverty exists is where people are oppressed either by other people (including governments) and cannot exercise their freedoms to create, or by their own limited thinking.

The good news is that they are not stuck there. **The greatest natural resource we have is the human mind and spirit. When people can believe in their own innate potential and have control over their own lives, they can prosper.** As long as we have enough freedom to educate and inform we can go around the socialist monopoly over education. As long as the socialist/progressive agenda is presented as *de facto* America, and the liberty agenda is demonized and minimized as radical, the socialists have an advantage. But that should not stop us. Our job is to remove the advantage by educating *individuals* and showing *individuals* the superiority of liberty.

The population of the dependent nation is fluid. No one is stuck there. Many want out of the dependent nation but do not know how to get out. But, like refugees, they trickle, one individual at a time, over the psychological border to join the parent nation when they begin to learn and to act on the truth that they are far more capable than they had been led to believe.

The German philosopher, Johann Wolfgang von Goethe, noted that, *"**None are so hopelessly enslaved as those who falsely believe they are free.**"* No one is free as long as his or her sacred time and energy are taken by force masquerading as law. Conversely, no one is free as long as he or she is dependent on others for his or her well-being.

One glance at any federal budget over the last seventy-plus years will show that the majority of government over-spending has been on "entitlement" programs. This is simply the transfer of money from one group of citizens to another. The idea that one citizen is "entitled" to the property of another is absurd on its face and antithetical to our founding principles. In fact, those who receive these transfers would never think to walk around to their neighbor's home, put a gun in their neighbor's face, and demand money. **And yet, this is exactly what they are hiring government to do when they vote for representatives who will do it for them.** If you think I'm exaggerating, try not paying your taxes and see what happens! Just joking. Don't try that.

Further evidence of these parallel nations is that the top fifty percent of all tax filers pay over ninety-seven percent of all taxes. The bottom fifty percent pay the other three percent. Only ten percent of that bottom fifty percent actually pays any income taxes at all.[1] Many receive tax "refunds" without having paid any taxes. These are statistics of only those who actually file income tax forms. Millions more—including illegal aliens, criminals, and other evaders—never even file, and all of them are eligible to vote. This is no accident. Irresponsible members of Congress have devised this system to grow their powerbase to ensure their reelection to positions of influence. It's also no accident that this voting bloc has given the mandate to such politicians to grow government into a monstrosity never before seen in history.

When such a small a percentage of citizens actually pay to support the legitimate functions of government there are not enough taxpayers to become outraged at all the wasteful, redundant, and unconstitutional programs. All adult citizens should have the privilege of helping to pay for government. When people actually have a stake in the functions of government they tend to pay more attention to its wrongdoings.

All reasonable people understand and accept that taxes are necessary and proper for the smooth running of any nation. The problem is that the means of collection of taxes is immoral under the income tax. And the wasteful use of taxes collected is mostly unconstitutional. On a very real level, we feel the pain and anger of having our sacred time and energy taken from us and then tossed into the wind by the billions, and even the trillions. The so-called "war on poverty" of the 1960's was a prime example. Trillions of dollars was transferred by government via taxation and redistribution to "solve" the problem of poverty in America. The end result was that government reduced marriage, increased out-of-wedlock births, and created the phenomenon of the poverty-stricken single-mother, by far, the largest dependent class in history.

Lest you think that the citizens of the parent nation are complaining about having to support the dependent nation let me explain something. Americans are the most charitable people in the world. Never in history has there been a nation whose individual citizens have voluntarily done and given more than the private, free citizens of the United States.[2] Few people in the world have not had their lives positively affected in some way by the charity of private citizens of America. This giving attitude comes from our Judeo-Christian heritage of taking care of the legitimately poor. Its genesis is in the Law of Moses in the Old Testament and in Jesus' reiteration of it in His "greatest" commandments: *"Love God with all your heart, with all your soul, and with all your mind…and love your neighbor as yourself."*[5] We may have lost sight of the Biblical origins of our generosity, but it is ingrained in our culture—at least in half of the culture. We do not need government to be Robin Hood. And we deeply resent being forced to "contribute" to government's wasteful schemes. Money taken by government could be money voluntarily given to charities that do the compassion thing much more efficiently.

Jesus said, "...*you have the poor with you always...*"³ and this is so. People will always be comparatively rich or poor. In Jesus' time, anyone who was born poor was more than likely to live his whole life poor and die that way. But since the founding of the United States, freedom of opportunity has been available for *anyone* to work his or her way out of poverty. I would say that ninety-nine percent of all so-called "rich" and middle-class folks in America started out as hardworking "poor" folks, but because they studied the right information, believed they could succeed, and took advantage of opportunity, they worked their way out of poverty. However, even though we live in a land that affords individuals the *opportunity* to achieve financial well-being, no one is guaranteed success.

The unacceptable condition of poverty *is* the incentive to climb out of it. As long as we make poverty acceptable, we take away the incentive to outgrow it. One of the books listed in the Ammunition section is Chris Gardner's, *Start Where You Are*. I highly recommend it to anyone who is tired of being poor. You may remember Chris Gardner as the homeless guy raising a son as he worked his way out of poverty. His story was portrayed in the book and movie, *Pursuit of Happyness*. Both of his books are inspirational resources for anyone!

A better way to go about "helping" the poor, as they work to help themselves, is by way of private charities, such as churches and other non-governmental entities. People are happy to give to help others when they see them trying to help themselves. But they resent it when people ask for a handout before they make a sincere effort, and they resent it when their income is taken by government to redistribute via inefficient and degrading "programs." James Madison had the same view. He said, *"The government of the United States is a definite government, confined to specified objects... Charity is no part of the legislative duty of the government."*

A free people do not want to be dependent or used by politicians. A free people are repulsed by the very premise that government should do anything for them other than protect their rights to life, liberty, and property. Just as the abolitionist movement struggled for decades to get people to recognize the inherent evil of slavery, we must struggle to get people to recognize the inherent evil of big government.

Many in the dependent nation are the manufactured poor. We've "manufactured" them by not teaching basic economics, real history, personal finance, and self-reliance. We perpetuate the dependent nation by not encouraging the citizens to think differently. We keep them dependent by allowing government to condescend to them. We reinforce their beliefs in their victimhood by not allowing them to participate in paying for government. When you think about the citizens of the dependent nation and the victim mindset they are stuck in, you cannot help but think that we do a disservice by enabling them to remain in victim-mode. Many who would otherwise work themselves out of poverty, because it is undesirable, get trapped in the web of social programs, where it is easy to remain stuck.

Benjamin Franklin said, *"I am for doing good for the poor, but I differ in opinion of the means. I think the best way of doing good to the poor, is not making them easy in poverty, but leading or driving them out of it. In my youth I traveled much, and I observed in different countries, that the more public provisions were made for the poor, the less they provided for themselves, and of course became poorer. And, on the contrary, the less was done for them, the more they did for themselves, and became richer."*

God has placed each of us in our own circumstances to stretch and grow us. If we shortcut that growth process, we will not reach our full potential. **If you try to "help" a chick escape its shell, you'll kill it.** That chick was designed to strengthen and grow as it pecks its own way out! I wonder, do we care enough to allow the chicks to strive and grow on their own? I wonder, are we compassionate enough to teach them self-reliance, goal-setting, and self-motivation? Do we care enough about our fellow citizens to begin once again to teach morality and good citizenship in schools? Do we care enough to demand that real American history, real economics, and responsible personal finance be taught in school, so that people can once again have a stake in the outcome of our future history? I believe we do care, and that the majority of us want others to prosper—not to just survive as dependents of the State.

Having stated the ideal, that the "poor" should be taken care of via private means and not by government (i.e., the taxpayers) and that they should be educated in the ways of self-reliance, please allow me to throw a little water on the edge of that fire. The fact is, so many people are dependent on government, and so many are counting on future dependence, the political reality is that a sudden switch to a self-reliant society just isn't going to happen. Far too many people vote simply for the goodies they will receive from government. And far too many politicians pander to that crowd.

The good news is that it is possible to reverse this downward spiral by turning the direction of our current national trend. The bad news is that it will take a few million more self-reliant people than we currently have.

We didn't get here overnight. It took a hundred years, from the institution of the income tax, to the New Deal, to the Great Society, to automatic withholding, to bailouts, to the debt tsunami that is happening now, to get us into this situation. The forces of socialism are so vast and well-funded (by our own money) that it will take a long time to cut the apron strings by which the dependent nation clings to the parent nation. Those apron strings *will* be cut, either voluntarily by the democratic process, or involuntarily by catastrophic economic collapse when we run out of other people's money.

Jesus tells us to love one another. If we wanted to obey that commandment, and if we were sincere, we would have to make the effort to share the principles of right thinking toward work, money, and government, while at the same time quietly giving where needed. If we were simply trying to *appear* to be compassionate to impress others with our goodness, we would devise socialist/progressive programs administered by a government that would *appear* to make life fair. This is what we're doing now.

Those of us who have climbed out of the ditch of poverty through hard work should be most willing to pass along this wisdom. We need to share our own experience, strength, and hope, so that others will know they need not be dependent on government. Essential to making opportunity available to *everyone* is to cut government down to its right size, and reduce the drain it puts on both nations. This allows for job and opportunity creation. In the next chapter, I'll spell out a simple plan to do just that.

Chapter Seven

The Five-Step Plan to Save America

"Any people anywhere, being inclined and having the power, have the right to rise up, and shake off the existing government, and form a new one that suits them better. This is a most valuable - a most sacred right - a right, which we hope and believe, is to liberate the world."

— Abraham Lincoln

"He has erected a Multitude of new Offices, and sent hither Swarms of Officers to harass our People, and eat out their Substance."

— Declaration of Independence, complaints against the King of Great Britain

Most good ideas are simple. They only seem complicated when naysayers start whining about how hard it will be to implement them. This chapter contains five simple steps to save America for future generations. All you have to do is find and support the right person who will vote for these five steps. You don't even need to break a sweat. All you have to do is use some of your time and energy to investigate candidates for Congress who will agree to stick to the simple Five-Step plan that I outline below, and then watch to make sure they do it!

In a letter to Elbridge Gerry, November 27, 1780, Samuel Adams said, *"If men of wisdom and knowledge, of moderation and temperance, of patience, fortitude and perseverance, of sobriety and true republican simplicity of manners, of zeal for the honour of the Supreme Being and the welfare of the commonwealth; if men possessed of these other excellent qualities are chosen to fill the seats of government, we may expect that our affairs will rest on a solid and permanent foundation."*

Throughout this book, I've referred to the wisdom of the Founders, and I've identified the source of their wisdom. **The reason we see little wisdom at work in government today is that we have reduced our election process to something of a beauty contest with a few sound bites and great choreography.** Little substance gets debated or even considered. Television simply does not have the time, nor do the talking heads on television have the capacity, to cut through the prepackaged veneer of candidates to get at their real character. Character is the issue, not looks or clever sound bites. Without godly character, a man or woman can never make wise decisions on our behalf.[1]

It has been wisely said that a politician looks at the next election, but a statesman looks at the next generation. How we need statesmen today who will focus on doing what is right and not what is easy! It's easy to promise voters you'll give them the moon and then raise taxes, borrow money, and increase the deficit to do it. It's easy to sit around and take pot shots at the other party, or dig up dirt on an opponent. It's easy to point out all the reasons good ideas won't work. Its easy to demagogue and denigrate and give slick speeches. These are the actions of small-minded people with short-term goals. That's the kind of politician you get when you don't do your homework before you vote.

In Appendix C, you'll see a sample letter that you can rewrite in your own words, to send to candidates before the elections of 2010 and 2012, to find out where they stand on this Five-Step plan. If they receive enough of these letters, they may get the message that the people care about what is going on in Washington.

If your letter gets ignored, or you get one of those cookie-cutter replies, you'll know to vote against them next time. If your representative or candidate for that office supports this plan (or something close to it), check out his or her positions on past issues to get a feel for his sincerity. **The last thing we need are more opportunists in Washington whose convictions flutter in the wind of influence.**

It is the duty of the people to be vigilant over government by making sure they elect people who respect the Constitution and will seek to prevent or reverse laws that are extra-Constitutional in nature. In a representative republic, when we vote for representatives, we loan them power to exercise wisely. If we end up with unwise representatives, it is our fault. As we have seen over the last several years, once elected, it is extremely difficult to get rid of them. The power of incumbency—media coverage, lobbyist's campaign donations, cronyism—serves to keep them in office no matter how anti-Constitutional their votes may be.

The power of the vote is a sacred trust and should not be manipulated or bought. Unfortunately, many voters today do not even know what the Constitution says, and worse than that, many others don't believe the Constitution is even relevant. The problems we face today, and the biggest threat to our future, are mindless voters who respond to the slogans and sound bites of candidates with little regard for substance, much less the original intent of the Constitution. One of the most outrageous crimes going on today is the government giving billions of dollars to one "community action" organization to actively recruit such voters.

Please pray that the God who caused this nation to be, and who guided our Founders in the writing of the Constitution, would bring forth 468 good men and women in 2010 who have a love for life and liberty and who will fight to defend the Constitution against *all* enemies, foreign *and* domestic. Some of those men and women are already in Congress, but they are in a distinct minority. If your congressperson or senator voted for the stimulus bill last October (2008), or any of the debt-ridden spending bills since then, or Cap and Trade, or nationalization of any industry or business, there is a very good chance that he or she does not subscribe to the principles outlined in this book.

You can find out how your current representative voted on these and other issues by going directly to their official websites at www.senate.gov and www.house.gov. Or you can go to www.cagw.org to see if your representative is on the list of "Porkers." If you doubt that spending is a problem, you can also see endless lists at that web site of your tax dollars being wasted in the millions and billions. On the positive side, you can see a list of "Friends of the Taxpayers" at www.ntu.org. These are congresspersons and senators who are already working on your behalf to stop wasteful spending. Find them in the "NTU Rates Congress" section. These two organizations are working on our behalf, and they need our support, along with the Heritage Foundation at www.heritage.org. If your representative has proven to be anti-liberty as evidenced by his or her votes on pork-barrel spending, your job will be to find a new representative or senator to support at the very next election.

Here are the five simple steps that the next Congress needs to take in order to reverse the downhill slide of this nation into socialism and perpetual debt:

The Five-Step Plan to Save America

Step One: Stop Borrowing

In the introduction, I explained what families have to do when they find themselves in debt. The first thing is to quit borrowing. Congress has to do the same, NOW! This is why we need strong, wise leaders who will not be influenced by all the cries of the dependent nation for their "special" needs, even the so-called need to bail out private companies that are considered "too big to fail."

What happens when government "bails out" anyone? The money to do so doesn't just come out of nowhere. It comes from you in five very destructive ways:

First, government has to borrow it, which decreases the amount of money available for banks to loan to help businesses expand, which would create new jobs. Debt has a depressing effect on the economy and on the psyches of people. When you're in debt, you feel the weight of oppression. I guess that's why God said, *"The borrower is slave to the lender."* (Proverbs 22:7)

Second, government needs the money to pay back that debt, so you get higher taxes, which further depress the economy. When people have less money to spend, businesses suffer loss of sales, which means businesses must lay off workers, which means workers collect unemployment, which comes from the government, which the government takes from the workers in the first place, and so on. It's a foolish cycle that would not exist if government would stay out of the free market.

Debt enslaves all of us. But most people don't want to think of themselves as slaves, so they just ignore the debt as it continues to grow like a monster. Since Congresspersons are not personally affected by their borrowing (in fact, they get rewarded by the constituents that they borrow for) they have little incentive to stop. And remember, even if our geniuses in Congress were to stop borrowing, the interest would continue to grow the debt out into eternity unless we pay it off.

The third way bailouts harm our nation is that when government gives or even loans money to a business, it comes with strings attached. Whoever gets bailed out has to now abide by government rules as to how their business is to be run. In this way, government "takes over" incrementally, and the business or industry becomes nationalized, or owned by government. Though the government may not own an industry outright, it effectively owns it, because government can mandate certain outcomes. Remember the definition of socialism in Chapter Five? It involves *"the vesting of the ownership and control of the means of production and distribution."*

Here's an example: When automobile companies are given huge government grants or loans to stay viable, do-gooders in government can tell them to make more energy-efficient cars. Sounds like a good idea. Who could be against more fuel-efficient, less-polluting cars? Well, how about the people who buy cars? Sales figures consistently show that the majority of people do not want little cars, even if they are fuel efficient. So, the government is effectively telling people what they should buy because of the types of cars they mandate, the tax credits they give for those who buy such cars, the tax they are imposing on gasoline, and so on. **In this way,** the free market becomes non-existent, and our freedom further erodes.

The fourth way bailouts hurt everyone is that, since the government will have to print the money to borrow, an excess amount of money is available on the market, which makes each dollar worth less. This means that if you have a hundred dollars in savings, ten years from now it may actually only buy what fifty dollars will buy today. When government prints more and more dollars, the value of each dollar is lessened. It's called inflation. **In this way, you are actually being robbed in the future by today's robbers, and the robbers are telling you that it is for your own good!**

The fifth, and what I consider the most destructive, way that bailouts hurt all of us is that they exist on the premise that only government can solve our problems, that government *should* solve our problems! When people are not allowed to suffer the consequences of their bad decisions, they never learn from them and continue to repeat them. That is exactly what is happening now and will continue until we put a stop to it.

Some will say that the banks and insurance companies that were bailed out in September 2008 had to be bailed out in order that they could continue to loan money to businesses who needed it to meet payroll and continue their operations so that innocent people would not be harmed by bank failures. The premise here is flawed. Guilt and innocence are not the issue. If it were, half of the House Banking Committee and Senate Finance Committees would be in jail, or at least would have resigned in shame. The issue is liberty. Free markets must be allowed to fluctuate according to market conditions. People have always gained and lost in the rhythm of the free market. Just ask anyone who had a 401k or an IRA, or any other investment. It's called life, and you deal with it.

If that sounds cruel, then you must think it is cruel to allow nature to take its course when species go extinct, which happens regularly, or it's cruel of us to not stop earthquakes, floods, or hurricanes. **It would have made much more sense to just allow the free market to settle, allowing the private sector to adjust to the job losses and bank failures that would have occurred.** The market would have recovered. It always has and it always will, if left alone! But instead, we socialized the whole mess in the name of "crisis" so that now all of us are paying for the incompetence of certain politicians. We know exactly who these politicians are, but as long as their constituents don't seem to mind their incompetence, and keep voting them back into office, there's not a whole lot that can be done about them. (In the case of the mortgage debacle, the market was not truly *free* because these very politicians I refer to, and President Clinton, had pressured banks to make risky loans, and then backed the banks with Fannie Mae and Freddie Mac, which means, with your money.)

Step Two: Cut Spending

Now, back to the example of a family trying to get out of debt. After they cut up their credit cards and quit borrowing, families must cut their budgets. Everyone has to tighten his belt. The same goes for government. Our new representatives must go to Congress with the resolve to cut every single area of government spending by ***at least ten percent***. Yes, even social security. Yes, even the military. At the very least, a waste of ten percent occurs regularly in every area of government. Anyone who has ever been in the military, or worked for the federal government in any position, knows that is a conservative estimate.

The average government worker gets paid more, and receives more benefits, than the average private sector worker doing a comparable job. I say *comparable* with tongue-in-cheek, because at least the private sector worker is being paid out of revenue his or her work generates for their company. Government generates no income, nor does it by produce anything that is salable in the free market.

Once you have cut all government budgets by ten percent, begin looking for redundant, unnecessary, and outdated programs that have been hanging around trying to justify themselves for years. I strongly urge the new Congress to pass a balanced budget amendment that would prevent future Congresses from spending more than they take in revenues, <u>without raising taxes to do it</u>! I realize this is an idea that has been shot down many times, but I believe that after the spending cuts and the Fair Tax have been in effect for a couple of years, it will become possible.

Step Three: Increase Income

Next, families must increase income to get out of debt and return to a sound financial footing. They may have to work two or three jobs. Children used to drop out of school to get jobs to help the family. They do whatever it takes to make more money.

Since government doesn't earn money, and we do not want higher taxes, the only way it can increase income is by broadening the base of collections. **Experience has shown over and over again that lower income and investment tax rates end up producing more revenue for government.** The way we have gotten out of all past recessions has been to reduce taxes. When more people are paying in, less in required of each taxpayer. Lower rates always means broader participation!

Make sure that your prospective new representative would vote to completely eliminate the capital gains tax, so people can once again invest in businesses, and businesses will be able to expand and produce more. When businesses grow, they need more people to do the jobs they create. When more people are working, more people are paying taxes. Then, if the taxes of those workers are lowered, they will have more money to spend and invest, which is a true "stimulus" to the economy. Of course, if lower income taxes result in more revenue to government, then it only makes sense that *zero* income taxes will bring in even more! Keep reading.

Step Four: Enact the Fair Tax

When the income tax is totally eliminated everyone has more money to spend on other things, and when the person spends, he or she pays the Fair Tax. *USA Today* recently reported that Federal tax revenue was down $138 billion, or thirty-four percent, from April 2008 to April 2009, because so many people have lost jobs.[2] Too bad. If we had a consumption tax, instead of an income tax, everyone, including all the foreign tourists, businesses, and corporations that purchase new goods and services in the United States would be paying taxes and we wouldn't have a revenue problem. All the drug dealers and mafia types would be paying the tax, and all the money parked overseas now to avoid income taxes would return to be invested in businesses that create jobs.

Is anyone on the Ways and Means Committee listening? No, their ways and their means are only what benefits them and their lobbyists.

What I like most about the Fair Tax is that it removes the element of coercion from the relationship of people to their government. I include the Fair Tax in this list of five simple steps because it is the single most powerful, and common sense, means of both creating jobs and bringing revenue to government. Under the Fair Tax, government will collect more revenue to get out from under the multi-trillion dollar albatross of debt that is threatening our very survival as a nation. The time has come for the Fair Tax. The Fair Tax is such a powerful and exciting growth engine for individuals, government, and the economy that the next chapter is devoted entirely to it.

Step Five: Set Up An Emergency Fund

When families get out of debt, they first establish an emergency fund so they won't have to borrow again in the event of inevitable emergency. Once we get the national debt paid off, government reduced down to the right size, and our spending under control, we need to be vigilant to not squander surpluses as previous Congresses have done. We must put into Congressional rules that a portion of annual revenues from the Fair Tax will go into a real emergency fund that will earn interest. This fund would be used only for meeting threats to national security. If we do not set aside such a fund, we'll end up borrowing again. A balanced budget amendment would make this emergency fund necessary, and a Fair Tax would make it possible.

This simple Five-Step plan above will work. But it will take time. Until then, allow me to state the obvious: Although the current income tax is immoral and will eventually be declared unconstitutional, it is nevertheless legal.

Never neglect to pay your legitimately owed taxes. As bad as the wasteful spending and poor decision-making is in Congress, it does not give you license to refuse to pay your legitimately owed taxes. What makes them legitimately owed is that the "lawmakers" in Congress established them. Though Congressmen do not have the moral right, they have the *legal* right to impose taxes. However, two wrongs don't make a right.

Jesus said, *"Render unto Caesar what is Caesar's, and unto God what is God's."*[3] As long as we are legally under this duly elected government, we are responsible to obey the laws that are passed, no matter how ignorant the laws are. The key to fixing this is to elect people of wisdom and understanding, rather than those with the ability to look and sound attractive.

The most important reason to pay your taxes is not that government mandates it, but that your refusal to do so can really mess up your relationship with God. **By trying to save a few bucks, you are telling God you don't really trust Him.** This is like building a dam in the river flow of your income. Everything we have comes from God. Do we not trust Him to continue to provide?

The way to handle your anger over government waste and fraud with your tax dollars is to work to elect responsible representatives. Let the injustice of the income tax and the abuses of the IRS and Congress be your continuing motivation to get rid of them all! This is the American way.

So, pay your taxes, while at the same time doing whatever you can to change the way they are collected and used. Just because we have a broken system does not mean you can abandon it. If you stay on the side of right, you will have the spiritual power to help fix it. If you go over to the dark side, not only will you legally lose, but you will give more power to the broken system. **Pay your taxes, and just be grateful that you don't get all the government you pay for!**

Chapter Eight

The Fair Tax

"Trust in the Lord and do good; dwell in the land, and feed on His faithfulness. Delight yourself also in the Lord, and He shall give you the desires of your heart."

— Psalm 37:3,4

"Evil prevails when good men do nothing."

— Edmund Burke

Here's your Quick Start Guide to the Fair Tax:

When passed and signed into law, the Fair Tax will completely eliminate the individual income tax, the alternative minimum tax, corporate and business income taxes, capital gains taxes, social security taxes, medicare taxes, self-employment taxes, estate taxes, and gift taxes. The Fair Tax will replace all of these punitive and regressive forms of taxation with a one-time, transparent, federal sales tax on new goods and services at the retail level. It will not be added to the current income tax, because the Sixteenth Amendment will be abolished as a condition of enactment of the Fair Tax.

The Fair Tax will create a wealth and job-generating machine that will itself solve many of our other problems. The financial benefits to individuals and the nation as a whole are numerous, and I don't have the space here to list them all. My main intention is to point out the moral imperative of having a tax system that is not punitive and condescending to free adults. The extreme economic benefits of a Fair Tax system are great, but the moral benefits are absolutely necessary.

There is not enough space in this book to thoroughly explain the Fair Tax, so please get more information about the Fair Tax at www.fairtax.org, or by reading the two books on the Fair Tax that are listed in Appendix A. These books were written by Congressman John Linder of Georgia, the primary sponsor of the Fair Tax in the House of Representatives, and Neal Boortz, a veteran radio talk show host who has passionately studied, explained, and promoted the Fair Tax for several years. My apologies in advance to these two men if I misspeak or confuse the issue in this brief summary.

"The FairTax" is before Congress now as The FairTax Act of 2009 — HR 25 in the House of Representatives and S.296 in the Senate. It is written with no space between the words, but I won't do that in this book. The current version of the Fair Tax bill may have to be modified in order to pass, but I have no doubt that some version of the Fair Tax is the solution to the current financial and moral crisis. The principles from which it comes, and the extensive economic research behind it, make it a model for the way we should go if we are ever going to return this nation to a place of liberty and justice for all. Our government was funded for over a hundred years on similar taxes. It is the right thing to do.

First, I like the Fair Tax because it is contingent on the repeal

of the Sixteenth Amendment, which gave us the income tax. The Sixteenth Amendment, passed in 1913, was one of the worst ideas to ever make it into law. It has brought fear and distrust into the relationship between the people and our government for almost a hundred years. A government that was designed to be by and for the people became the people's enemy through the Sixteenth Amendment.

Second, I like the Fair Tax because it is un-intrusive and non-coercive. We only pay taxes when we choose to spend money on new retail goods or services, not on what we earn. It allows workers once again to keep their entire paychecks! It doesn't tax retirement income or distributions from retirement funds. Savings and investment income would no longer be taxed.

Forty-five states already have a sales tax system. The other five will come along when they see that state governments will receive one quarter of one percent of federal sales tax collections. Merchants who collect the tax will also receive the same percentage for their efforts in handling the money.

Having lived in Florida—a state without an income tax—for most of my life, I can tell you that it makes perfect sense for everyone who lives here, and everyone who visits here, to help support the functions of state government. It is fair that everyone who lives in and visits the United States, enjoying the benefits of its infrastructure and protections, should help pay for it.

A third reason I like the Fair Tax is that drug dealers, criminals, and everyone who now earns a living in the "underground" economy will no longer be able to avoid doing their part to support government. Why? Because they buy retail goods and services. Right now, the IRS estimates that there is a multi-trillion-dollar underground economy that is not paying any tax at all. The Fair Tax eliminates all loopholes and tax evasion tricks. This will bring in billions to the treasury of the United States.

The Fair Tax

Over thirteen trillion dollars has been invested in foreign banks so that investors can avoid paying capital gains taxes in the United States. Under the Fair Tax there would be no more capital gains taxes. Imagine what would happen if all, or even just half, of that money came back to American financial institutions when the capital gains tax was abolished! So much more investment would be made in American businesses that the unemployment rate would go to zero (assuming we quit counting those who do not *want* to work). We would probably have to import more workers; but hey, that's a minor problem compared to what we're facing now.

If you're worried about "the poor" getting hurt by the Fair Tax, there is a provision for that also. Taxes on basic necessities like food are neutralized by a monthly advance refund, called a "prebate." With the prebate, everyone (including the lowest income earners) would get an advance refund of taxes to be paid monthly on the purchase of subsistence items, such as food and medicine. One drawback to this is that the dollar amount per prebate is based on family income, which brings government back into your private business to determine the amount of your prebate.

In addition to the prebate, a payroll tax would no longer exist—that is, no longer would employers have to be collectors of income, social security, and medicare taxes. That means *all* workers will be taking home at least twenty-five percent more in their paychecks! **Lower income earners will make out much better under the Fair Tax, both financially and morally,** since they will no longer have the fruit of their labor taken out of their paychecks and they will be exempted from paying the Fair Tax on the basic necessities of life.

The fifty percent of people who now pay no income taxes would finally be contributing to the federal treasury, which would give them a stake in their own government. This would greatly improve their motivation to learn about liberty and limited government! However, since everyone would receive the prebate, those whose incomes are below the level of the prebate would effectively be paying no taxes. We would probably spend the first few years under the Fair Tax with the same forty percent of Americans paying no taxes at all. However, as the job market would no doubt improve due to the increased economic activity, increased investment in United States stocks with no capital gains, and the relocation of foreign corporations to the United States to take advantage of no income tax, wages would go up because of competition for workers. The "poor" would then have true opportunity to work themselves out of poverty, which means they will become frequent Fair Tax payers as they buy more goods and services.

The best news about the Fair Tax, and the fourth reason I like it so much, is that the Fair Tax abolishes the IRS and removes the power of intimidation from bureaucrats who supposedly work for us! Right now, it costs Americans a minimum of *six billion hours* a year just to fill out the forms and do all the calculations with the current tax code. Speaking of forms, there are five hundred twenty-six of them—all made for your convenience in complying with the income tax code.

When the income tax was initiated in 1913, the tax code consisted of a whopping four hundred and two pages. Today, the tax code is fifty-five thousand pages! The cost to individuals and businesses is over two hundred sixty-five billion dollars a year in accounting fees, just to "comply" with this massive system. This "unfunded mandate" is an indirect form of theft—it's effectively another tax. **When private citizens are forced to spend so much of their lives "complying" with government, they are essentially servants of the state.** Any government that can take your time and energy like this is immoral. This immorality would be completely gone in a Fair Tax system. The cost of merchants' collection and accounting would be covered by their percentage gained.

Under the Fair Tax, we would regain all that sacred time and energy we are currently spending just to keep track of our finances for the IRS. That time and energy could remain in the economy working to build businesses and create jobs. All savings and investments would go through the roof, because interest earnings on what you save would not be taxed. Your *interest* would earn interest tax free, making the compounding of that interest astronomical over time. You would no longer have to make decisions about investments based on what Big Brother is going to do to you. Individuals and businesses spend millions of hours a year making tax avoidance decisions. Think about it: **To have to spend *any* time trying to figure out how to avoid being punished by government is proof that you are not really free.**

What has always angered me the most about the income tax is the way our "representatives" in Congress have used it to manipulate our behavior. To get us to buy homes, they "gave" us a home mortgage interest deduction. To get us to invest in alternative energy, to donate to certain charitable organizations, or to do this or that with our money in order to save on our tax bill, they passed their little rules to cause their desired outcomes. Anyone out there feel like a child? **Deductions, credits, exemptions, allowances, and other forms of condescending manipulation do not belong in a nation of free individuals.** Our government has no business even knowing how we earn, save, or spend the fruits of our labor. When the Fair Tax is implemented, you will no longer have to even consider the tax consequences of your decisions.

I believe the aversion to paying taxes of any kind will cause many of us to just save more and spend less. Isn't this what we should be doing anyway? When you save money, you have more control of your life and your future. You will eventually spend the money and pay the sales tax when you do, but only after you've accumulated all that untaxed interest! Also, when citizens and foreigners begin stashing their money in United States banks, because the interest on savings will not be taxed, a massive increase in money will be available for banks to lend for building and growing the economy. This environment would make the United States once again the preferred place to invest. Job creation would explode. **The Fair Tax is the single most powerful anti-poverty initiative we could ever implement because good paying jobs would proliferate.** If there is anyone in Congress who truly cares about the poor, and about providing opportunity for everyone, you can discover them by their stance on the Fair Tax.

When the capital gains tax is eliminated, individuals and businesses all over the world will start investing in American businesses again, and capital will flow into the United States at an unprecedented level. Companies will want to locate their businesses in the United States where labor costs and living conditions will be much more competitive with other countries. Then, when these same investors buy products in the United States they will pay the Fair Tax.

Don't make the mistake of assuming that the Fair Tax would be on top of what we are paying already. No. The Fair Tax replaces all other federal taxes. I know I've said this before, but it needs to be repeated many times because most Americans naturally assume that the government has a trick up its sleeve when they start talking tax reform, and historically that has been an accurate assumption. But the Fair Tax bill, as written, is a clean bill. It ain't reform, it's revolution!

Be careful of the argument that this tax would be added to the current price of goods and services, so that a refrigerator that costs one thousand dollars now would then cost one-thousand three hundred dollars. No. Let's get this right. **All of the income taxes that people currently pay are embedded in the current cost of everything you buy.** The people who assembled the refrigerator had to pay their income taxes, as did everyone else who supplied parts for the refrigerator, as did the people who made the parts, and the miners who brought up the iron ore, and so on. All of the income taxes that all of these people and businesses had to pay are already included in the price of the refrigerator. Once income taxes are not a factor, market competition would drive the cost of the refrigerator down, so that the twenty-three percent Fair Tax would bring the price close to the current level. Don't forget that the reasons United States manufacturing has gone overseas is to take advantage of the lower costs of paying those overseas workers because taxes in the United States made wages too high. When we have eliminated the embedded income taxes of everyone along the line of production, we too will have a lower cost for our products, making them more competitive in the U.S. and around the world.

The main point is this: by eliminating all taxes on personal income, we will make a giant leap toward self-reliance and freedom. We will have more personal savings, which will earn interest, which will mean more savings, which will mean more future income, and so on. In addition to each of us finally having a chance to become wealthy through the traditional means of saving our un-taxed, hard-earned money, that money that we invest will be borrowed by businesses to expand, which will create more jobs. Everyone wins. Even government!

Far too many aspects of the Fair Tax exist for me to include them in this book, and I don't want to be the sole source of your information about it. So, I encourage you again to go to the web site www.fairtax.org or to get the books to have your questions answered. You can also go the Library of Congress web site at www.thomas.loc.gov and look up H.R.25 or S.296. You can see a portion of the Congressional findings on H.R. 25 in Appendix B. Also, please check out the list of sponsors and co-sponsors of these bills at www.encouragingwordpress.com. Anyone who has already signed their names to the bill has proven they have wisdom and courage.

This effort to eliminate the income tax is a moral imperative. It has to be done, whether it is the Fair Tax or something similar

that replaces it. The rightness of the cause is what will propel it forward to success. You will probably read many arguments against the Fair Tax from people who benefit from the current system or who don't even pay taxes because they've learned how to beat the system. Many politicians and lobbyists benefit from the complexity of the income tax, so they don't like something that's simple, fair, and transparent. They'll say the Fair Tax "hurts the poor," "it will devastate the economy," and a lot of other sophistry (sophistry is the use of clever-sounding, but misleading arguments). The fact is, no one can rightfully say that the current income tax system is either sane or moral. All attempts to "simplify" it have only caused more insanity. You can't keep trying to fix a house that is built on a bad foundation!

ADJUSTMENTS TO THE FAIR TAX

I do have some improvements to the Fair Tax that I want to suggest here. Remember what follows is not currently part of the Fair Tax bill that is currently before Congress. Economic and political circumstances in the United States have changed dramatically since the bill was introduced in 1999 by Representative John Linder from Georgia. So, I have some adjustments to propose. If you are a current supporter of the Fair Tax in Congress please feel free to use these ideas. I don't care who gets credit for them, as long as we get the bill passed!

1. **Cap the Fair Tax Rate at Ten Percent**. When the designers of the Fair Tax studied its impact on the economy, society, and government, they determined it would be best to use a twenty-three percent tax rate, because they figured it would be easier to pass if it would bring in the exact amount of revenue that is now being raked in via the income tax. The fear was that people are so addicted to their handouts and programs, and Congresspersons are so addicted to their power, that any attempt at cutting spending first would shoot the bill down right away. Their reasoning was that it would be much

easier, politically, to simply replace the income tax with the Fair Tax and leave spending cuts as a separate issue. However, the landscape of America has changed dramatically since the bill was first introduced in 1999.

The catastrophic spending since September 2008 makes it imperative that spending be cut first. This is why cutting spending was step two of the Five-Step Plan to Save America in the previous chapter, with the prerequisite being to replace most of the current Congress with new, more Constitution-minded folks. With the right people in Congress, we would no longer be manipulated into maintaining federal spending levels. Remember that Step One of the Five-Step Plan is to immediately quit borrowing. Step Two is to cut spending and reduce all federal budget items by at least ten percent across the board. This has to be done first, or we will never get out of the financial hole we're in.

My strong suggestion to members of Congress is to cut so much spending that the rate required for a federal consumption tax be no more than ten percent, and that the rate be cast in stone unless a super-majority in the House votes to increase it. A percentage of that ten percent should be designated to go to an emergency fund so that the federal government will not have to borrow in times of national emergency ever again. This ten percent rate would leave room for states and localities to also adopt their versions of the Fair Tax.

2. **Make it Optional**. In consideration of the fact of our parallel nations, and the reality that some will simply not *like* the Fair Tax for various reasons, let's make the Fair Tax optional. With the technology we have today, there is no reason we could not give people a choice. **All who prefer the Fair Tax would be completely removed from the income tax rolls, and all those who prefer the current income tax system could simply remain in the system.** This means that those who choose the income tax would still have the individual income tax, withholding taxes, social security taxes, medicare taxes,

and self-employment taxes. They would still have to keep all their receipts, pay their accountants, maintain files for seven years, and file those forms every April 15th to comply with their preferred tax method. However, since the currently embedded income taxes would no longer be in products they buy at the retail level, they would still have to pay the embedded Fair Tax, (because the embedded taxes would be roughly the same as the embedded income tax they pay now. But, they could continue to pretend that there is no embedded tax, just as they have been doing all their lives.) It's so simple! Oh yes, I almost forgot—their savings accounts, stocks, bonds, gifts, and estates would all be subject to the same income taxes as today, and they'd still have to file by April 15th or be subject to penalties and audits. Then when they die, they'd have to pay the death tax. **Now that's what I call pro-choice!**

3. **Give It An Appropriate Title**. Change the Fair Tax name to "The Civil Rights Act of 2011." No other act in the history of Congress will have ever provided more civil rights than this one. The term "civil rights" in *Webster's New World Dictionary* is defined as, *"those rights guaranteed to the individual by the 13th, 14th, 15th and 19th Amendments to the Constitution of the United States and by other acts of Congress; esp., the right to vote, exemption from involuntary servitude, and equal treatment of all people with the respect to the enjoyment of life, liberty, and property and to the protection of law."* In fact, all of the people who support civil rights of any sort should be totally on board with the Fair Tax, because it would be the most wide-sweeping civil rights reform since abolition of slavery.

4. **Spread the Wealth**. Another improvement to all of our lives would be for the state and local governments to replace all of their income, property, and other taxes with a ten percent Fair Tax—for example, seven percent to the state, and three percent to local governments. This would bring the total Fair Tax to twenty-percent, but that's far better than the over fifty percent that most people pay

now in combined federal, state, and local taxes. The goal would be to completely eliminate the carrots and sticks that the federal government uses to influence sovereign states to "comply" with federal mandates. Since states would be handling the collection of the Fair Tax they could keep their share, in addition to the handling fee, before it get to the feds. The last thing we would want to see is the federal government in charge of returning revenue to the states!

So, who could possibly be against this Fair Tax? Well, here are a few:

1. **Lobbyists**. The opponents of the Fair Tax will be all those who currently make their living from the complexities of the more than seventy thousand-page tax code that no human understands. The people who have made themselves experts in parts of the code, such as corporate taxes, estate taxes, employment taxes, etc., have set themselves up in lucrative businesses deciphering and manipulating the code for profit. Others spend full time lobbying Congress to manipulate the code for their clients' benefit. These tax experts do not want to give up their lucrative jobs. They are relatively few in number, but they wield enormous amounts of cash with which to influence the votes of Congress. This is another powerful reason we must replace the majority of people who are now in Congress with new people, especially those who support the Fair Tax.

2. **Manipulators**. Many in Congress gain their power by manipulating the tax code to their benefit, for social engineering, and for kickbacks in the form of campaign contributions. For example, the mortgage industry would want to maintain the tax deduction for home mortgage interest, so they will be doing whatever they can to influence the members of Congress to not support the Fair Tax. Many other special interests contribute money to politicians in exchange for tax code loop hole for their industries, or even for individual companies.

Many politicians will only give up this source of power and income if they are forced to by being voted out of office. The Fair Tax is the most effective form of campaign finance reform we could adopt!

3. **Non-profit organizations**. Charities and religious organizations will cry loudly against the Fair Tax, because charitable contributions will no longer be tax deductible. Think about it. How can you have an income tax deduction when you don't have an income tax? Besides, under the Fair Tax, people will be taking home all of their paychecks. If charitable givers had grown accustomed to tithing on their net income, guess what? There is no net income any more. It's all gross income. People who give a regular percentage of their income to churches, ministries, and other charitable organizations will end up being able to give more. This means more money can be received by charitable organizations that are supported by regular givers—unless givers were giving only to get the tax deduction… People who give only to get a charitable deduction on their income taxes should look closely at the benefits of not having to justify any giving. Jesus said,

> *Take heed that you do not do your charitable deeds before men, to be seen by them. Otherwise you have no reward from your Father in heaven. Therefore, when you do a charitable deed, do not sound a trumpet before you as the hypocrites do in the synagogues and in the streets, that they may have glory from men. Assuredly, I say to you, they have their reward. But when you do a charitable deed, do not let your left hand know what your right hand is doing, that your charitable deed may be in secret; and your Father who sees in secret will Himself reward you openly.*[1]

I know that not everyone will subscribe to this sort of thinking, but even those who don't will recognize the value to character building. Once the benefits of the Fair Tax overall are understood, I doubt that anyone would see the loss of the charitable tax deduction as a worthwhile reason to oppose the Fair Tax. If you are one who gives or receives charitable donations just because of the tax deduction, you may want to "run the numbers," both fiscally and spiritually.

3. **Busy-bodies**. Unfortunately, some people just like to talk and to hear themselves talk, even before they know all the facts. They'll blog, Twitter, spam, Facebook, send letters to editors, and call television and radio talk shows to spout opinions as if they were facts. You can't do much to stop them. If they don't have enough sense to study a subject before they express opinions about it, well, what can I say? We do have freedom of speech.... Maybe some Fair Tax supporter who is especially creative could make a cartoon video that would explain the Fair Tax facts in an entertaining way to those people who won't take the time to listen or read a book....

4. **Demagogues**. The same types of people who have told us every election year for at least fifty years that the R's, if elected would take away social security, or that the D's would spend us into bankruptcy, would still be around. They'll try to scare people into opposing the Fair Tax out of fear of losing a government handout. This *will* happen. This is exactly why we need to find and support patriots with hearts for the next generations of Americans, not their own petty careers.

In 1773, when the colonists held the Boston Tea Party, it was over a duty that the British had imposed on the tea they imported to America. In other words, before a shipment of tea could be unloaded, a tax had to be paid to the British government. At that time, there was no income tax. Taxes were collected as duties or imposts (taxes on imports or exports), levies (specific taxes assessed for various purposes), and excises (taxes on specific items, like tobacco, liquor, etc.).

Outrage at the British for imposition of these taxes was enough to cause the colonists to fight for independence from Great Britain. **Imagine any one of the Americans of that time living today and having to pay a tax on their income! A revolution would have taken place long before now!**

Article I, Section 8, of the Constitution does give Congress the *"Power to lay and collect Taxes, Duties, Imposts, and Excises..."* All of these taxes were on products and businesses. Of course, these taxes were passed along to citizens by the businesses thus taxed. It was only common sense, and everyone understood the purpose of such taxes to be the support of legitimate government functions. The idea of a direct tax on the income of private citizens was unthinkable. These indirect taxes were the "original intent" of the word "taxes" by the signers of the Constitution.

My primary objection to the income tax is that it is immoral and unconstitutional. Immoral, because it legalizes the taking of private property by force. Unconstitutional, because it violates The Fourth Amendment, which states, *"The right of the people to be secure in their persons, houses, papers, and effects, against unreasonable searches and seizures, shall not be violated...."* The violation of these rights is what galls me. And every citizen should be equally angered.

I've never been audited. (Although I won't be surprised to be after this book is published!) But I have had to take time away from work to drive fifty miles to the nearest IRS office, when summoned, to prove that I was right and they were wrong on an subcontractor issue. I was losing money by complying with the IRS's demand that I present myself to them, while the people confronting me had all the time in the world to deal with me. They got paid, got a retirement income, got health care, and the security of a government job as they dealt with me. They even took their union-mandated breaks as I waited for them in their lobby!

Since I was self-employed and did not have the luxury of a government job, every minute that I had to spend dealing with that issue I was losing income which would have paid my bills, paid for my health insurance, and paid into a retirement fund for me and my family. When a tax arbitrator finally ruled that I was right and they were wrong, did they offer to reimburse me for time and energy taken from me without cause? Of course not!

The Fifth Amendment says that no person shall be *"deprived of life, liberty, or property, without due process of law; nor shall private property be taken for public use without just compensation."* **If the government can force you to spend your time dealing with their mandates, they are essentially depriving you of your life, liberty and property.** I know this sounds like a petty argument to some, especially those who have an employer paying them as they deal with government. But to me, and millions like me, this kind of coercion evokes righteous indignation. The IRS has all the time and money in the world to crush me or any other citizen simply by an arbitrary demand for justification of any of a million details of the tax code! Just the idea that my own government, which I pay for, can legally cause me to do *anything* (when I haven't broken the law) is enough to get me riled up. Sometimes I wonder why my fellow citizens are so impassive about government having such power as this. Especially the descendants of slaves. I think it has to do with a lack of understanding about both the Constitution and certain spiritual laws.

The Constitution also says in Article I, Section 9, that *"**No capitation, or other direct Tax shall be laid, unless in Proportion to the Census or Enumeration herein before directed to be taken.**"* Past Supreme Courts have held that the Sixteenth Amendment, establishing the income tax, did not really violate Article I, Section 9 under the reasoning that the income tax was not really a direct tax on the people. To most common sense citizens, a tax that comes out of your pay before it even reaches your hands is pretty ***direct***!

Further common sense thinking would conclude that if the income tax is *not* a direct tax, why would you need an amendment to the Constitution to establish it? **You wouldn't need an amendment to do what is already legal.** The Supreme Court has been wrong before and has been overturned by subsequent courts, as in Dred Scott, Plessy, and prohibition, to name just a few. These and other cases clearly illustrate that, as long as we're in the business of "balancing" the Court by skin color, gender, and ethnicity, we should also have a roofer or a plumber, or two, on the court to give it some proper balance. Surely the Sixteenth Amendment could then be overturned on the basis that is a *direct tax*, and therefore unconstitutional. But since it would be a long, long time until we can get such a common sense Supreme Court, we'd better just take the matter into our own hands and get rid of it ourselves, and here's how:

The people can force Congress to repeal the Sixteenth Amendment to make way for the Fair Tax. In fact, the adoption of the Fair Tax is contingent on the repeal of the income tax. There are two ways to get this done. Article V of the Constitution states:

> *"The Congress, whenever two thirds of both Houses shall deem it necessary, shall propose Amendments to this Constitution, or, on the Application of the Legislatures of two thirds of the several States, shall call a Convention for proposing Amendments, which, in either Case, shall be valid to all Intents and Purposes, as part of this Constitution, when ratified by the Legislatures of three fourths of the several States, or by Conventions in three fourths thereof, as the one or the other Mode of Ratification may be proposed by the Congress."*

This means that we have to either get two-thirds of both houses of Congress to vote to propose an amendment, or two-thirds of the state legislatures to ask Congress to call a national convention to propose amendments. Once an amendment is proposed, it has to be ratified by either three-fourths of the state legislatures, or ratifying conventions in three-fourths of the states must approve it. This is how prohibition, the Eighteenth Amendment, was repealed by the Twenty-first Amendment.

The Supreme Court has stated that ratification must be within "some reasonable time after the proposal." Beginning with the Eighteenth Amendment, it has been customary for Congress to set a definite period for ratification. In the case of the Eighteenth, Twentieth, Twenty-first, and Twenty-second Amendments, the period set was seven years, but there has been no determination as to just how long a "reasonable time" might extend. I'd say, the quicker the better for the Twenty-eighth. However, we have to make sure that the votes are there in the state legislatures to ratify the Twenty-eighth, which would repeal the Sixteenth. Otherwise, the issue would be dead for many more years as patriots continue their attempts to wake people up.

With a proper understanding of why and how, this insidious power of the income tax can be removed. This *can* be done. This *will* be done. All you have to do is vote for representatives in both the Congress and your state legislature who support the Fair Tax, then *insist* that they act to ratify a new amendment that would repeal the 16th Amendment.

As I have stated, I have nothing against paying taxes. I do it regularly and on time. I'm not a tax "protester." I have the duty and privilege to do my part to support government in its *legitimate* functions. **I merely want the government to get out of the insane income tax business and adopt a clear, simple, honest, Constitutional consumption tax.** That's all. The very assumption that government can cause me to spend my time and energy "complying" with its demands for detailed information is wrong. "Compliance" means submission, which rubs me the wrong way, and which brings me to the spiritual aspect.

The Bible says that Christians, are to submit to the authorities: *"Let every soul be a subject to the governing authorities. For there is no authority except from God, and the authorities that exist are appointed by God."*[2] **In the case of the United States, the *authority* is the Constitution, and all aspects of the law that are in accord with it.** There is no doubt that the Constitution's authority was appointed by God. It is our *duty* to see that no extra-Constitutional authority is imposed on us by our elected representatives, and that no judge reads into the Constitution what is not there.

Furthermore, there is a huge difference between submitting because I'm forced to, and submitting out of devotion. I submit to God because I'm devoted to Him. I submit to my wife because I'm devoted to her. I submit to my country because I'm devoted to it. I *choose* devotion. It cannot be forced on me. This is why those whose job it is to interpret law, must be devoted to upholding the original intent of the Constitution as the basis of the law. **Determining original intent is not difficult to do, but it is crucial.** You need look no further than the writings of the Founders for the intent of their positions.

Many will fight to implement other agendas before the Fair Tax for a variety of reasons. One of those reasons is that some feel that returning Tenth Amendment power to the states and the people is more pressing than a Fair Tax. However, the Fair Tax removes the incentive for federal intervention in your state. **When state sales tax collectors are sending the Fair Tax collections to Washington, that should be the extent of the states' dealings with the federal government.** Federal government would have no power over the state governments, because the Federal government would not be sending money to the states to prop them up and then laying down conditions for the states to meet.

We also have many people now who want term limits imposed on Congress, so we can get rid of the really bad actors who have caused so much trouble through their arrogance and ignorance. But, think about it this way: what if we do manage to find five hundred and thirty-five common-sense, originalist patriots to man Congress? (Or even just a few!) We'd be really upset if term limits forced them to leave before they got the job done! So, let's work on the Five-Step Plan first. Then, if we don't get enough patriots on board, we can talk about term limits.

Of course the ideal term-limit is the voluntary one, like George Washington exercised. Politicians should just term-limit themselves out of a love for country and a sense of humility.

The fight to replace the punitive income tax with the Fair Tax, or any alternative consumption tax, is primarily a moral battle.[3] **This imperative is similar to the abolitionist movement of the 1800s and the civil rights movement of the 1900s.** We need only awaken the innate sense of right and wrong in our fellow citizens to make the 2000s the century of the rebirth of individual liberty and personal responsibility. This will not be easy. But let's take the attitude of President Washington, who said, *"Let us raise a standard to which the wise and honest can repair; the rest is in the hands of God."*

CHAPTER NINE

GET BACK TO THE CONSTITUTION

"It is the duty of the patriot to protect his country from its government."

— Thomas Paine

"…When they constituted us as a nation by ratifying the Constitution and the amendments that have followed, our forefathers gave up only certain of their powers, enumerating them in a written constitution. We have allowed those powers to expand beyond all moral and legal bounds—at the price of our liberty and our well-being. The time has come to return those powers to their proper bounds, to reclaim our liberty, and to enjoy the fruits that follow."[1]

— Dr. Roger Pilon

I call the flag on the cover of this book, "The Get Back! Flag," because the people who display it will be telling government to "get back" before it gets bitten! They will also telling government to "get back" to its Constitutional limits, by doing the things listed on the flag. I'm sure many more demands could be added, but I believe these are the most pressing issues today. I believe that if we persevere in demanding that our representatives in Congress act on the eighteen items listed on the "Get Back!" flag, we will be ensuring American liberty and justice for at least the next hundred years. **Who knows what future generations will do? But they won't have the freedom to do anything worthwhile if we do not take a stand for them now.**

On September 25th, 2005, Dr. Roger Pilon, founder and director of the Cato Institute's Center for Constitutional Studies in Washington, D.C., addressed the U.S. Senate Committee on Homeland Security and Governmental Affairs, Subcommittee on Federal Financial Management, Government Information, and International Security. His address was entitled, "THE UNITED STATES CONSTITUTION: From Limited Government to Leviathan." You can see his entire speech at www.cato.org, but I excerpt a portion of it here with permission:

> "...We come, then, to the nub of the matter. Search the Constitution as you will, you will find no authority for Congress to appropriate and spend federal funds on education, agriculture, disaster relief, retirement programs, housing, health care, day care, the arts, public broadcasting—the list is endless. That is what I meant at the outset when I said that most of what the federal government is doing today is unconstitutional because done without constitutional authority. Reducing that point to its essence, the Constitution says, in effect, that everything that is not authorized—to the government, by the people, through the Constitution—is forbidden. Progressives turned that on its head: Everything that is not forbidden is authorized." "...when powers or rights are expanded or contracted not through ratification

> *but through elections and the subsequent actions of elected officials, and the courts fail to check that, the Constitution is undermined and the powers thus created are illegitimate. That happened when the New Deal Court bowed to the political pressure brought on by Roosevelt's Court-packing threat. And that paved the way for powers that have never been constitutionally authorized by the people—for illegitimate powers, that is—and for the accompanying loss of rights."* [1]
> [Emphasis mine.]

This is why we need to elect people that respect and abide by the Constitution. We most urgently need to replace the people who serve on the Senate Judiciary Committee with Constitutional scholars who believe in adhering to the original intent of the Founders, and who will not approve judge nominees who have a view of the Constitution as old-fashioned, or worse, "living." To do this, we need an overall Constitutional education of the people. We don't need any more "get out the vote" drives. **We need to "get out the education," then the vote will take care of itself!**

The "Get Back!" flag shown on the cover of this book is available to purchase at www.getbackflag.com. By displaying this flag, either as a 3'x5' flag, a window decal, or on a T-shirt, you will be sending a message to government and to your fellow citizens that you are on-board with the revolution to return government to the size and scope originally intended in the Constitution and to return America to its founding principles. I'm not out to start another political movement or party. God knows, we don't need another party to take our votes and our money to throw around the political playing field.

But what we do need is a *voice* as individuals expressing individual and authentic outrage. It is my intention to give voice to the millions of patriots who just want government and the sycophantic media to hear their anger and frustration over "business as usual" in

Washington. It is the *individual* that matters. It is the *individual* that lives and works and pays taxes and gives their very existence to the state through coercive taxation.

Personal freedom. Personal responsibility. Individual rights. These are the foundations of America that we must regain if we are to survive as a nation!

For far too long, government has responded to noisy whine-groups that have organized to intimidate politicians to act on their behalf. They whine for government to do this and that for them, and they get it. Now it's time for the *individual* to take over. We're not asking for anything. We're taking back our country with Constitutional action. We don't need to organize. That would be contradictory to the whole idea of individuality. **It is the individual that votes.** You can belong to any party, or no party at all. It's you, the individual, who will decide and vote, based on your principles and values. It's you who will contribute or not to individual candidates, not parties. Beware of partisans who tell you you're "throwing away your vote" if you don't align with a political party. Parties are the *cause* of the inane and never-ending, child-like bickering over how to spend the citizens' money.

This will be the era of the self-reliant, independent individual. The time has come. The elections of 2010 will give us an opportunity to get rid of the tax and spenders in the House of Representatives, and by election time in 2012, and 2014 we should be able to replace all of the Senators with Constitutionalists. Those who are now supporting tax increases in every form, from the income tax, to cap and trade, to socialized medicine, to bail outs of everyone who is "too big to fail," to the scam of climate change initiatives, will find themselves out of power. Then the politicians will know that the era of individual responsibility and freedom is upon them.[2] And we'll all have a good laugh on election day to see the pundits and the pollsters baffled at what happened!

An added benefit to the "Get Back!" flag is that with every flag purchased in whatever form, you will be buying a carbon offset. I will personally cause a tree to be planted on your behalf for every flag purchased. You can emit all the CO_2 you want with no more sense of guilt or shame that you are breathing, driving, or living. Is this a great country, or what? You can rest assured that a lovely tree, expressing itself as a free individual being on planet earth, will be offsetting your carbon dioxide emissions with its oxygen emissions. You should get one for every member of your family and all your friends, especially the ones who are concerned about carbon dioxide.

Below you will see a brief explanation of the demands on the "Get Back!" flag. Not everyone will agree with all of the demands listed on the flag, and still others will have demands that are not on the flag. But I believe that most common sense Americans will agree that most of the principles represented by the flag are fundamental to the workings of a free nation.

It is frustratingly ironic that free people have to take so much of their sacred time and energy to reel in their government and force it to "get back" to performing only the functions spelled out in the Constitution. Nevertheless, that is where we find ourselves. So, if you find yourself in agreement with at least half of the standards listed on the flag, I encourage you to display it. Once we have new, Constitution-minded representatives we can work out the priorities of these standards:

GET BACK TO THE CONSTITUTION

We want Congress to pass no law that is not in accord with the original intent of the Constitution. We want judges at all levels to be accountable to the Constitution, as written. We want the executive branch of government to uphold and enforce the provisions of the Constitution. We want schools at all levels to teach the original intent of the Constitution as the law of the land.[3]

RESPECT PROPERTY RIGHTS

We want government to completely respect all property rights and to abide by its Constitutional authority to protect private property from theft and seizure by anyone, including itself. Property includes all real estate, personal property, all income, all savings and investments, and all that an individual owns by natural right and law.[4]

DOWNSIZE GOVERNMENT

In addition to cutting government programs, we want the actual numbers of people employed by government to be reduced dramatically. We want the government employees' union disbanded so that they remember that they work for the people. We want Congress to reduce every budget item by a minimum of ten percent, across the board, with no exceptions. This can easily be done just by trimming the fat in every area of government. We want all programs and agencies that are no longer doing anything but trying to justify their existence to be eliminated. The list of such programs and agencies is too lengthy to add to this book, but they can be readily found on such websites as **www.cagw.org**, **www.ntu.org**, and **www.heritage.org**, among others.

REPEAL THE 16TH AMENDMENT

The income tax should be abolished and the Internal Revenue Service dismantled under the provisions of the Fourth Amendment: *"The right of the people to be secure in their persons, houses, papers, and effects, against unreasonable searches and seizures, shall not be violated…"*, AND under the provision of Article I, Section 9, *which says in part,* **"No capitation, or other direct Tax shall be laid,** AND under the provisions of the 28th Amendment, which will establish the Fair Tax.

ENACT THE FAIR TAX

We want the Fair Tax enacted to completely replace the income tax and to begin collecting the revenue necessary to pay off the debt and fund only the legitimate functions of government. We want any excess revenue after the debt is paid off to go into an emergency fund so that government will not have to borrow in the future to deal with national threats.

PROMOTE PERSONAL RESPONSIBILITY

We want government to quit bailing out individuals, businesses, and especially failed government programs. We do not want government providing or funding services which are the responsibility of the individual and private organizations. We believe health care is more efficient and available when provided by the free market in response to supply and demand. Government funding of health care, as in the case of Medicare and Medicaid, is what has caused health care to become as expensive as it has. We want government to get out of the business of spending taxpayer's dollars to warn people not to do things that may be harmful to themselves. We want government to cease doing for people what they can and should do for themselves, with exceptions in extreme cases of mental or physical limitations, but only after all private help is exhausted.[5]

ENFORCE CLEAN ELECTIONS

We want all government funding of so-called "community activist," get-out-the-vote efforts to cease. We want government to stop funding advertisements to encourage people to vote. Voting is a private matter, not to be either encouraged or discouraged by government. We want government to stay completely out of the campaign finance realm by first repealing any existing campaign finance laws, rules, and programs. We want government to be totally neutral when it comes to political elections. We want law enforcement to investigate and prosecute any and all attempts at election fraud, regardless of infraction location, party, or race.

ALLOW ENERGY INDEPENDENCE

We want American oil and natural gas companies to have access to any natural deposits within our national borders and offshore limits. We want proven nuclear power companies to be allowed to build and provide energy from safe nuclear sources. We want anyone to be able to access alternative sources of energy, such as solar, wind, tidal, etc., but without government funding, tax incentives, or regulation. Government has no role in private industry, except to ensure safe operation where the public is at risk. We want government to receive no tax on energy, except the portion of sales that generates the Fair Tax.

ENFORCE SECURE BORDERS

We want illegal immigration stopped immediately and illegal aliens to be deported. We also want access to legal immigration to be made easier so that any law-abiding person may have easy legal access to the American dream of freedom.

RESPECT STATE SOVEREIGNTY

We want the Tenth Amendment adhered to by both state and national government. The Tenth Amendment states, *"The powers not delegated to the United States by the Constitution, nor prohibited by it to the States, are reserved to the States respectively, or to the people."* We want each of the fifty states to be "sovereign," having jurisdiction over its own residents, programs, and prosperity. The Fair Tax collection fee shall be a revenue source for each state depending on how efficiently each state runs it.

PROTECT INDIVIDUAL RIGHTS

The individual has priority over government. In all interaction with private citizens, the people's servants in government will give complete respect and preference to individuals over other policies and procedures. In the case of suspicion of wrongdoing, citizens should be given the benefit of any doubt. No law for "the greater good" should take priority over an individual's right to life, liberty, and property.[6]

NO REGULATION WITHOUT REPRESENTATION

No regulation should ever be imposed by any government agency without having first gotten specific approval of the people *through their elected representatives* who would be accountable for the regulation. This includes the Environmental Protection Agency, the Department of Natural Resources, the Department of Energy, the Department of Education, and all other government agencies and entities.

REMEMBER GOVERNMENT IS A SERVANT

Every government employee, whether elected, appointed, or hired, should be required to recite the oath of office as a condition of employment. When any such person is found to have violated, or to have caused a violation of any part of this oath, this will be grounds for removal from government service:

> *"I do solemnly swear that I will support and defend the Constitution of the United States against all enemies, foreign and domestic; that I will bear true faith and allegiance to the same; that I take this obligation freely, without any mental reservation or purpose of evasion, and that I will well and faithfully discharge the duties of the office on which I am about to enter, so help me God."*

Article VI of the Constitution requires all Representatives, Senators, executive officers, judicial officers, and several state legislatures to affirm support for the Constitution. By living up to the oath, government servants are most likely to remember that they are servants and are to be guided in their duties by the Constitution first. Since the oath requires government servants to defend the Constitution against all enemies, "foreign and domestic," the servant should first defend the Constitution against himself or herself, then against his or her own party.

CUT SPENDING

We want budget cuts of *at least* ten percent at every department, agency and program of government, no matter how painful it may seem. Every family in America has to cut spending when times are tough. Government is bound by the same moral law to not spend more than it takes in. Tax increases are not the answer to government spending. Cuts across the board are the answer. Then we want complete elimination of non-essential programs and agencies.

PAY OFF THE DEBT

Yes, the United States has always had debt, but it was miniscule in comparison to the eleven trillion dollar debt we have now! The only reason we have so much debt is that government has reached beyond its Constitutional boundaries and attempted to solve problems it was not designed or intended to solve. Wise representatives will be the people who know that problems are not solved by throwing money at them. Just because there has never zero debt does not mean that there cannot or should not be zero debt. Investors can always find private stocks and bonds to invest in.

BALANCE THE BUDGET

We don't need an amendment to the Constitution to do this,

but it may become necessary. It is really up to the people to elect representatives who will vote to keep the executive branch sane in its budget requests from year to year. This does not mean raising taxes so that government can spend more and still be within its "budget." It means keeping spending down. Period.

PROTECT FREE MARKETS

Government's job is to protect citizens from harm by internal or external enemies. Government should recognize that by intervening in the free market, *it* is an internal enemy. Government should never provide subsidies for any industry, person, or union, whether though protectionism, bailouts, direct payments, or monopolies. Government should have no monopoly on education. This means that education should be allowed to compete in the free market for students and funds, and that parents should have complete control over curriculum.

TERM LIMIT YOURSELF

The only way we can have term limits with meaning is if honest and dependable candidates term-limit themselves by making a compact with voters to do so. If these voluntary term limits are not honored, and the incumbent attempts to run for reelection to the same office, in spite of their own pledge, voters will know they are not worthy of reelection.

Chapter Ten

Right Revolution

"When the righteous are in authority, the people rejoice: but when the wicked rule, the people mourn."

— Proverbs 29:2

"We the People are the rightful masters of both Congress and the Courts—not to overthrow the Constitution, but to overthrow the men who pervert the Constitution."

— Abraham Lincoln

I went to China in 2006 with the Christian orphan ministry, Grace and Hope for Children.[1] I had been there twelve years earlier, and I was shocked to see the rapid pace of growth that had gone on since I had been there last. Among the many changes, the people seemed to have changed the most. A vibrant energy seemed to be buzzing all the time. Night and day you could go out on the streets and meet people buying, selling, and transporting goods via every vehicle you can imagine—from huge trucks, to water buffalo pulling carts, to bicycles piled ten feet high with goods.

Over the eleven years since I had previously been there, the Communist Party had loosened restrictions on private industry so much that the economy was booming. New stores, residential buildings and compounds, railroads, and highways seemed to have sprung out of the ground like so many bamboo shoots after a rain. People had incentive to work and accumulate property, and the resulting prosperity was everywhere to be seen.

When I was born in 1953, only about six hundred million people were living in China, and poverty was rampant there. The Communists were devastating the country with centralized control. What kid growing up in 1950s America did not hear, *"Eat all your vegetables, because there are starving children in China"*? I didn't quite understand how eating my broccoli was going to help some kid on the other side of he world, but it must have worked, because now there are one and a third billion people in China, and I don't know of any that are starving.

Out of that one and a third billion, only about three hundred million are what we could call middle class. Of course, that middle class is equal to our entire population now. The remaining billion are living on very little, but they have hopes for economic improvement. Many are self-employed as small street vendors, craftsmen, farmers, and a thousand other professions. They are feeding themselves and they see the prosperity that capitalism is bringing to their country. There is much hope for more and more liberty, which will mean more and more prosperity.

I don't bring up China to compare it to the United States, because the two can't be compared—the cultures are so vastly different. But the human response to oppression is the same everywhere, and the response to opportunity is the same. The bustling crowds of intent faces going about their various and diverse jobs gave me a glimpse of what it must have been like for the immigrants who first came to the United States from other countries to find opportunity to advance economically. **Where freedom exists people have hope.**

The Chinese people are no different than Americans. Don't make the mistake of thinking they are in lock-step with their government. They want all the same things we want out of life—peace, security, prosperity, and hope for the future. The Chinese I met were very focused on achievement and advancement within their new free market. Many were devout Christians. Many were self-employed, selling everything from fresh vegetables and ducks to clothing and machinery in little shops on just about every street. Every individual and family took care of themselves, and in so doing, they were all having their needs met in the free market. The government is still there, but the people always find a way to work around it. Americans could learn from the poor Chinese who are working their way into self-sufficiency.

People-led decentralization. That is what is saving China. **This decentralization is not only saving China, but causing it to become the next world superpower.** As America declines into big-government socialism, Communist China is rising into capitalism. But it wasn't led there by its government. The people led the government there. They took matters into their own hands, and the sheer masses of people practicing private industry became too big for government to control. When the government loosened restrictions on markets, it was because they had no choice.

Now, China has become so wealthy, it is propping us up by loaning us money. When they buy our Treasury bills, that is exactly what they are doing. They get a piece of paper saying we'll pay them back with so much interest. But now the Chinese are worried that they may not get paid back.

Several times in this book, I have quoted Proverbs 22:7: *"The borrower is slave to the lender."* **By allowing government to impose** its "soft tyranny" of taking care of our every need, we have slowly but surely arrived at the place where we no longer own ourselves. Sadly, most Americans don't even seem to notice, and many Americans who do notice don't seem to even care. Sadder still, many prefer it this way. We are becoming what China used to be—totally controlled and manipulated by a central government. The only way to get out of this situation is to just take charge.

We could learn from the communist experience in China. We could learn from the former residents of the Soviet Union. We could learn from the European socialist states and even from the failures of socialized medicine in Great Britain and Canada. But the out-of-control spending in Congress and the results of the election in 2008 cause me to wonder if there are enough freedom loving people left in America to actually make a difference.

Every American who reads this book should see this as a wake-up call. **We have allowed our politicians to spend us into slavery.** No, we do not have physical chains on our ankles. But we have the invisible chain of debt on our left leg and one of big government on the other. Both of them have been forged out of dependency. Half of us voted for it, and the other half allowed it. Parallel nations. Parallel paths. Parallel chains.

I am ashamed to say it, but I think the Chinese see the lack of integrity in our government, and they are afraid that Congress *will* default. When you owe someone money, they have power over you. They either have physical collateral or a legal claim to your future earnings. When they are afraid you aren't going to pay them back, they feel a strong sense of ownership of whatever you have that is valuable. What would that be to the Chinese? I don't know. Maybe they'll ask us to get rid of our missile defense programs. Maybe they'll want Alaska. Maybe McDonalds. (Hey, we could give them Washington DC! Just an idea….)

In reality, all that creditors want is their money. How will they get their money out of the United States? The most logical way is to just take it in payments over many years. Where will the money come from to make those payments? You guessed it. From you, your children, and your grandchildren and great-grandchildren, and so on. The borrower is slave to the lender. It's only fair.

What is not fair is that the people in Congress who borrowed all the money are acting as if they had nothing to do with it. What is not fair is that the same people who caused this problem are trying to "fix" it. Lord, help us! At the very least, every person who sits on the House Finance Committee should be voted out in 2010. Every person who voted for the so-called "stimulus packages" should be voted out in 2010.

We must find four hundred sixty-eight freedom-minded citizens to populate our Congress in 2010. That's four hundred thirty-five in the House of Representatives and thirty-three in the Senate this year. Then in 2012 we can replace another thirty-three, and in 2014, we can get rid of the last of the big spenders, even though, by then they should be in a powerless position.

It is up to us. **Those that are there now aren't going to willingly change or retire.** We have to take the initiative NOW. If we don't, the future looks dim for your children and grandchildren and their children, and so on. The crushing burden of debt we face now can only be overcome if we can elect the people who will stop the borrowing NOW. Stop the spending NOW. Cut government programs NOW. Enact the Fair Tax NOW, so that we can pay off the debt and get ourselves back into financial health. Then we can reform the education system to make sure this sort of regression into centralized government control does not happen again.

During the revolution of 1776, roughly one-third of the citizens of the colonies wanted independence from Great Britain. Another third sided with the enemy. And the remaining third remained uncommitted, on the sidelines. Even fewer actually fought to gain our freedom for us. In this day, when we need at least fifty-one percent of the vote, one-third won't work. **We have to educate the majority of citizens before it is too late.** It may be too late already. But I have faith that God will prevail if we will turn to Him for wisdom and quit trying to solve problems by printing money! Pray that the current Congress will come to its senses and reject socialism. Pray that God will enter and change their hearts and minds. Pray that the leadership in the House and Senate, and the President will be led to wise, Godly counselors who can show them the wisdom that He has already given us through the Founders. They can reverse course. They must reverse course, or at least stop the destruction-bound forward motion of the ship of State.

The entire Old Testament is the story of man's relationship with God. God is faithful, constant, and rock-solid. He gave the people His Law to guide them, but each generation had to go its own way. One generation would heed the words of God and prosper. They were called righteous. Then the next generation would dismiss the words of God and suffer. They were called evil. Sometimes God would let the entire nation languish in captivity for several generations, but eventually a new generation would repent and restore the relationship with God. One of these cycles stands out as a picture of modern-day America that we had better pay attention to:

It had been fifty-five years since a righteous king had ruled. The two previous kings had forgotten all about God, and had even worshiped false gods. Most of the people who had lived under the righteous King Hezekiah had passed away, and no one was left who remembered what it had been like during his reign. One day, as the priests carried out the new King, Josiah's, command to clean up and restore the old temple, one of them found Moses' Book of the Law, which had been lost for generations. He dusted it off and took it to the king, and said, "Look what I found!" *(Give me a break, Bible scholars, I'm making a point!)*

When the priest read the Law to King Josiah, the king was horrified, and said, "Great is the wrath of the Lord that is poured out on us, because our fathers have not kept the word of the Lord, to do all that is written in this book." He then commanded the people to return to adhering to the Law, and they prayed and sacrificed and tore down the false gods they had built, and did all that they could to restore their relationship with God. And it looked like it was working, but then the King died and was succeeded by two evil kings in a row. It was too late. The people did not know the real God or how to worship Him, because they had not been taught. Their fathers and grandfathers had turned to other gods, and had forgotten the source of their power as a nation. So their enemies attacked and killed all the young men, and all the people were hauled off to Babylon to be slaves for seventy years. You can read the whole story in 2nd Chronicles, chapters 33 – 36 to find out more.

In a similar way, Americans have forgotten their Constitution because it has not been taught, and Congress has loaded our government with completely unconstitutional programs, agencies, and spending that is not constitutionally authorized. We have forgotten the admonitions of our Founders and turned to human understanding, politics and technology for leadership, and we are reaping the disastrous results. Am I saying we should become a theocracy? Of course not! But I am saying that if we had not rid our schools of Biblical teaching, and if more Americans were at least aware of where our freedoms come from, we would not be in this mess.

America was not made free or prosperous by government. **No nation has ever taxed, spent, or legislated itself into greatness.** Just the opposite. Many have fallen due to misuse of the people's resources. It was God who gave us our nation, then He gave us the Constitution to preserve it! If we cannot return government to the principles and values of the Founders and the original intent of the Constitution, our suffering will be well deserved.

Our slavery to the debt owned by foreigners is upon us. No, the Chinese won't carry us away. They have enough people. But they, and others who have bought our debt, will rightfully own the fruits of our labor through exorbitant taxes for many, many years to come, perhaps the rest of the Twenty-first Century. And no one in America will be free as long as this debt exists.

What will you tell your grandchildren when they ask what you did in the Revolution of 2010-2012? Whose side will you say you were on? Did you fight for the freedom of the next generations, or did you tune out and let others do the fighting for you? In 1775, Patrick Henry gave his now famous *"give me liberty or give me death"* speech to the Virginia House of Burgesses. His last seven words are well known, but I quote an earlier portion of his speech here, because it foreshadowed what we are going through now:

> *"Sir, we are not weak if we make a proper use of those means which the God of nature hath placed in our power. The millions of people, armed in the holy cause of liberty, and in such a country as that which we possess, are invincible by any force which our enemy can send against us. Besides, sir, we shall not fight our battles alone. There is a just God who presides over the destinies of nations, and who will raise up friends to fight our battles for us. The battle, sir, is not to the strong alone; it is to the vigilant, the active, the brave. Besides, sir, we have no election. If we were base enough to desire it, it is now too late to retire from the contest. There is no retreat but in submission and slavery! Our chains are forged! Their clanking may be heard on the plains of Boston! The war is inevitable--and let it come! I repeat it, sir, let it come."*

My friends, in this current revolution, you do not have to shoot anyone. **All you have to do to begin taking your life and our country back, is to educate yourself and encourage your fellow**

Right Revolution

citizens to educate themselves. Pass along one or more of the resources in the Ammunition section. Join or simply support one or more of the organizations that are fighting for your freedom, such as Americans for Fair Taxation, National Taxpayer's Union, The Heritage Foundation, The Cato Institute, The 912 Project, and others. Become educated and educate. Do not depend on government schools or even government-funded universities for this. If they were teaching truth, we wouldn't be in this predicament! The very least you can do is pass along this book to a friend, relative, or co-worker. And if you're really committed you'll fly the "Get Back!" flag or put the flag decal in a window, so that when people ask what it is all about you can tell them.

The American dream is really the dream of every human being. The Founders wanted to preserve this dream for future generations so they gave us a great Constitution. The Constitution they devised was, we believe, divinely inspired. Yes, it has had to be amended along the way. That's how we righted the wrongs of slavery, the women's vote, prohibition, and others. We can also right the wrong of the income tax, socialistic big government, and the national debt in this way. The beauty of the Constitution and the genius of the Founders is that they provided for wrongs to be righted by non-violent means. And, just in case government goes too far, they gave us the Second Amendment.

Jesus said the greatest commandment was, "*You shall love the Lord your God with all your heart, with all your soul, and with all your mind and You shall love your neighbor as yourself.*"[2] Who is your neighbor? It is your spouse, child, grandchild, friend, and every stranger you meet. Your neighbors are the unborn children, the legal immigrants seeking opportunity, and the soldiers who will fight and die for future generations. Our neighbors are also those who came before us and fought and died to maintain our freedom.

Do we dare do nothing and leave future generations with the

tyranny of debt, oppressive income taxes, and an out-of-control government, when all we have to do is pass around a book or two and vote? Is this going to be the generation that gave it all away in exchange for a little security? Thomas Jefferson said, *"Anyone who trades Liberty for security deserves neither Liberty nor security."*

I know I have painted a bleak picture. But, dear friend, it is much worse than I have been willing to paint. The enemies of freedom surround us. But, the good news is that what seems impossible to man is possible for God.³ In the Bible, there is a story about the nation of Israel being surrounded by enemies. It goes like this:

> *"Now the king of Syria was making war against Israel… Therefore he sent horses and chariots and a great army there, and they came by night and surrounded the city. And when the servant of the man of God [the servant of the prophet, Elisha] arose early and went out, there was an army, surrounding the city with horses and chariots. And [Elisha's] servant said to him, "Alas, my master! What shall we do?"*
>
> *So he [Elisha] answered,* **"Do not fear, for those who are with us are more than those who are with them."** *And Elisha prayed, and said, "Lord, I pray, open his eyes that he may see." Then the Lord opened the eyes of the young man, and he saw. And behold, the mountain was full of horses and chariots of fire all around Elisha. So when the Syrians came down to him, Elisha prayed to the Lord, and said, "Strike this people, I pray, with blindness." And He struck them with blindness according to the word of Elisha.*
>
> *Now Elisha said to [the Syrian soldiers] "This is not the way, nor is this the city. Follow me, and I will bring you to the man whom you seek." But he led them to Samaria. So it was, when they had come to Samaria, that Elisha said, "Lord, open the eyes of these men, that they may see." And the Lord*

opened their eyes, and they saw; and there they were, inside Samaria!

Now when the king of Israel saw them, he said to Elisha, "My father, shall I kill them? Shall I kill them?" But he answered, "You shall not kill them. Would you kill those whom you have taken captive with your sword and your bow? Set food and water before them, that they may eat and drink and go to their master." Then he prepared a great feast for them; and after they ate and drank, he sent them away and they went to their master. So the bands of Syrian raiders came no more into the land of Israel."[4]

I started this book off with a story about George Washington praying in the snow. The God to whom General Washington prayed is still here. We just need to turn to Him. Pray that He will raise up strong, honest, wise lovers of liberty once again to serve in government. Pray that He will cause dishonest journalists to fail in their attempts to obscure and twist the truth. Pray that millions of our fellow citizens will become aware of the threat to themselves and to future generations by excessive government. Pray that they will turn out and vote for liberty.

Like Washington and the King of Israel, we too are surrounded. Victory seems impossible. But we have unseen forces coming to our aid. They are the angels of freedom, truth, personal responsibility, integrity, faith, and love. They ride on chariots of fire, and they will not abandon the battle, if we don't.

Powerful forces have risen and fallen throughout history in vain attempts to conquer, control, and enslave men. The forces we face today — the national debt, the income tax, socialism, progressivism, and poor education, all caused and supported by our own government — are probably more powerful than army that has ever existed. Our fellow citizens are blind to the threat posed by those forces, and have been deluded into clinging to government as a benevolent god.

But, "those who are with us are more than those who are with them." Let us win this battle peacefully, through education, then at the ballot box. Let us defeat them with love. Then let's bring those we have defeated into a feast of prosperity, self-reliance, and freedom. We will prevail if we do not give up. We will prevail if we do our part and trust God to do His.[5]

Appendix A

Ammunition

This is not a bibliography, but a list of many good resources for learning about liberty. All of these books are available at **www.encouragingwordpress.com**. The DVD's are available at amazon.com, and some of the books are in audio form at **www.audible.com** and other on-line stores.

- *A Patriot's History of the United States: From Columbus's Great Discovery to the War on Terror,* by Larry Schweikart and Michael Patrick Allen
- *A Conflict of Visions, Revised Edition (2007)* by Thomas Sowell
- *America – A Call to Greatness,* by John W. Chalfant
- *America Alone: The End of the World as We Know It,* by Mark Steyn
- *America: The Last Best Hope (Volumes I & II),* by William J. Bennett
- *American Heroes,* by Oliver North
- *America's Victories: Why the U.S. Wins Wars and Will Win the War on Terror,* by Larry Schweikart
- *The American Patriot's Almanac,* by William J. Bennett and John Cribb
- *The American Soul,* by Jacob Needleman
- *The Anti-Federalist Papers and the Constitutional Convention Debates,* by Ralph Ketcham
- *An Inconvenient Book,* by Glenn Beck
- *Applied Economics,* by Thomas Sowell
- *Basic Economics,* by Thomas Sowell
- *Benjamin Franklin: An American Life,* by Walter Isaacson
- *Blackbelt Patriotism,* by Chuck Norris

- *The Book of Virtues,* by William J. Bennett
- *The Broken Hearth: Reversing the Moral Collapse of the American Family,* by William J. Bennett
- *Bulldozed: 'Kelo,' Eminent Domain and the American Lust for Land,* by Carla Main
- *Capitalism and Freedom,* by Milton Friedman
- *The Case Against the Fed,* by Murray N. Rothbard
- *Censorship: The Threat to Silence Talk Radio,* by Brian Jennings
- *Climate Confusion: How Global Warming Hysteria Leads to Bad Science, Pandering Politicians and Misguided Policies that Hurt the Poor,* by Roy Spencer
- *The Constitution of the United States of America, with the Bill of Rights and all of the Amendments; The Declaration of Independence; and the Articles of Confederation,* by Thomas Jefferson
- *Common Sense: The Case Against an Out of Control Government,* by Glenn Beck
- *Crash Proof: How to Profit From the Coming Economic Collapse,* Peter D. Schiff
- *Debt Free Living,* by Larry Burkett
- *Democracy in America,* by Alexis de Tocqueville
- *The Deniers: The World Renowned Scientists Who Stood Up Against Global Warming Hysteria, Political Persecution, and Fraud,* by Lawrence Solomon
- *The Fair Tax Book: Saying Goodbye to the Income Tax and the IRS,* by Neal Boortz and John Linder
- *The 5,000 Year Leap,* by Cleon Skousen
- *Do the Right Thing,* by Mike Huckabee
- *Economic Facts and Fallacies Fallacies,* by Thomas Sowell
- *Economics in One Lesson: The Shortest and Surest Way to Understand Basic Economics,* by Henry Hazlitt
- *End the Fed,* by Ron Paul
- *FairTax: the Truth: Answering the Critics,* by Neal Boortz and John Linder

Appendix A

- *48 Liberal Lies About American History: (That You Probably Learned in School)*, by Larry Schweikart
- *Free to Choose*, by Milton and Rose Friedman
- *God and Government*, by Charles Colson
- *The Heritage Guide to the Constitution*, by Edwin Meese
- *His Excellency, George Washington*, by Joseph J. Ellis
- *The Holy Bible*, by God
- *The Housing Boom and Bust*, by Thomas Sowell
- *John Adams*, by David McCullough
- *The Law*, by Frederick Bastiat
- *Learning About Liberty*, by Cato University
- *Let Freedom Ring* by Sean Hannity
- *Lies That Go Unchallenged in Media & Government* by Charles Colson
- *Libertarianism*, by David Boaz
- *Liberty and Tyranny: A Conservative Manifesto*, by Mark Levin
- *Liberty versus The Tyranny of Socialism: Controversial Essays*, by Walter E. Williams
- *The Making of America*, by Cleon Skousen
- *Meltdown: A Free-Market Look at Why the Stock Market Collapsed, the Economy Tanked, and Government Bailouts Will Make Things Worse*, Thomas E. Woods, Jr.
- *The Moral Compass*, by William J. Bennett
- *More Liberty Means Less Government: Our Founders Knew This Well*, by Walter E. Williams
- *Our Country's Founders*, by William J. Bennett
- *Own Yourself: A Challenge to Strong, Brave, Intelligent Young Men*, by C. Jesse Duke
- *Original Intent: The Courts, the Constitution, and Religion*, by David Barton
- *Power to the People*, by Laura Ingraham
- *The Real Benjamin Franklin*, by Andew M. Allison
- *The Real George Washington*, by Jay A. Parry
- *The Real John Adams*, by Andrew M. Allison

- *The Real Thomas Jefferson,* by Andrew M. Allison
- *The Revolution: A Manifesto,* by Ron Paul
- *Restoring the Lost Constitution: The Presumption of Liberty,* by Randy E. Barnett
- *The Richest Man In Babylon,* by George S. Clason
- *The Road to Serfdom,* by F. A. Hayek
- *Self-Reliance,* by Ralph Waldo Emerson
- *1776,* by David McCullough
- *Slouching Toward Gomorrah,* by Robert Bork
- *Start Where You Are,* by Chris Gardner
- *The Social Contract,* by Jean-Jacques Rousseau
- *Success Mastery Academy,* by Brian Tracy
- *The Spirit of America,* by William J. Bennett
- *Taking America Back: A Radical Plan to Revive Freedom, Morality and Justice,* by Joseph Farah
- *The Ten Big Lies about America,* by Michael Medved
- *The Tenth Amendment and State Sovereignty: Constitutional History and Contemporary Issues,* by Mark R. Killenbeck
- *Total Money Makeover,* by Dave Ramsey
- *Two Treatises of Government,* by John Locke
- *Uncle Sam's Plantation: How Big Government Enslaves America's Poor and What We Can Do About It,* by Star Parker
- *Unstoppable Global Warming: Every 1,500 Years,* by S. Fred Singer and Dennis T. Avery
- *The Wealth of Nations,* by Adam Smith
- *We The People: The Story of Our Constitution,* by Lynne Cheney
- *What's So Great about Christianity,* by Dinesh D'Souza
- *Why American History Is Not What They Say: An Introduction to Revisionism,* by Jeff Riggenbach
- *Winners Never Cheat,* by John M. Huntsman
- *You're Broke Because You Want to Be,* by Larry Winget

Appendix A

DVDs

- *The American Heritage Series (2009),* by David Barton and John Pevoto
- *The Foundations of American Government,* by David Barton
- *Media Malpractice,* by John Ziegler,
- *Rediscovering God in America,* by Newt Gingrich
- *Spirit of the American Revolution,* by David Barton
- *The Great Global Warming Swindle* by various scientists
- *The New Economic Disorder: Strategies for Weathering Any Crisis While Keeping Your Finances Intact, by* Dr. Larry Bates
- *We The People: The Character Of A Nation,* by Gateway Films

WEBSITES WITH MORE AMMUNITION

- American Center for Law and Justice — www.aclj.org
- Americans for Fair Taxation — www.fairtax.org
- American Solutions — www.americansolutions.org
- The Avalon Project — www.avalon.law.yale.edu
- CATO Institute — www.cato.org
- Citizens Against Government Waste — www.cagw.org
- Climate Truth — www.greatglobalwarmingswindle.com
- Club For Growth — www.clubforgrowth.com
- Heritage Foundation — www.heritage.org
- Human Events — www.humanevents.com
- Ludwig von Mises Institute — www.mises.org
- National Debt Clock — www.brillig/debt.clock.com
- National Review — www.nationalreview.com
- National Taxpayer's Union — www.ntu.org
- Stand to Reason — www.str.org
- The 9/12 Project — www.912project.org
- U.S. Term Limits — www.termlimits.org
- Young Americas Foundation — www.yaf.org

APPENDIX B

Congressional Findings on the Fair Tax

The following is an excerpt from the table of contents of H.R. 25, outlining the reasons for abolishing the income tax and then listing the reasons for replacing it with the Fair Tax. You can see the entire bill at **www.thomas.loc.gov**. LOC stands for Library of Congress.

SEC. 2. CONGRESSIONAL FINDINGS.

(a) **Findings Relating to Federal Income Tax- Congress finds the Federal income tax--**

(1) retards economic growth and has reduced the standard of living of the American public;

(2) impedes the international competitiveness of United States industry;

(3) reduces savings and investment in the United States by taxing income multiple times;

(4) slows the capital formation necessary for real wages to steadily increase;

(5) lowers productivity;

(6) imposes unacceptable and unnecessary administrative and compliance costs on individual and business taxpayers;

(7) is unfair and inequitable;

(8) unnecessarily intrudes upon the privacy and civil rights of United States citizens;

(9) hides the true cost of government by embedding taxes in the costs of everything Americans buy;

Appendix B

(10) is not being complied with at satisfactory levels and therefore raises the tax burden on law abiding citizens; and

(11) impedes upward social mobility.

(b) **Findings Relating to Federal Payroll Taxes- Congress finds further that the Social Security and Medicare payroll taxes and self-employment taxes--**

(1) raise the cost of employment;

(2) destroy jobs and cause unemployment; and

(3) have a disproportionately adverse impact on lower income Americans.

(c) **Findings Relating to Federal Estate and Gift Taxes- Congress finds further that the Federal estate and gift taxes--**

(1) force family businesses and farms to be sold by the family to pay such taxes;

(2) discourage capital formation and entrepreneurship;

(3) foster the continued dominance of large enterprises over small family-owned companies and farms; and

(4) impose unacceptably high tax planning costs on small businesses and farms.

(d) **Findings Relating to National Sales Tax- Congress finds further that a broad-based national sales tax on goods and services purchased for final consumption--**

(1) is similar in many respects to the sales and use taxes in place in 45 of the 50 States;

(2) will promote savings and investment;

(3) will promote fairness;

(4) will promote economic growth;

(5) will raise the standard of living;

(6) will increase investment;

(7) will enhance productivity and international competitiveness;

(8) will reduce administrative burdens on the American taxpayer;

(9) will improve upward social mobility; and

(10) will respect the privacy interests and civil rights of taxpayers.

(e) **Findings Relating to Administration of National Sales Tax- Congress further finds that--**

(1) most of the practical experience administering sales taxes is found at the State governmental level;

(2) it is desirable to harmonize Federal and State collection and enforcement efforts to the maximum extent possible;

(3) it is sound tax administration policy to foster administration and collection of the Federal sales tax at the State level in return for a reasonable administration fee to the States; and

(4) businesses that must collect and remit taxes should receive reasonable compensation for the cost of doing so.

(f) **Findings Relating to Repeal of Present Federal Tax System- Congress further finds that the 16th amendment to the United States Constitution should be repealed.**

APPENDIX C

SAMPLE LETTER TO CONGRESSIONAL CANDIDATES

Dear Sir or Ma'am,

I understand that you are running for Congress. Congratulations on your ambition and good luck with your campaign.

I'm writing to suggest that you read C. Jesse Duke's book, *Spread this Wealth (and Pass this Ammunition!)* before you get too far along. I also suggest that you read Jim Demint's book, *Saving Freedom*, Glenn Beck's, *Common Sense*, or Mark Levin's, *Liberty and Tyranny*.

If you agree with the ideas expressed in these books, you have my support. Send me a yard sign, a bumper sticker, or a petition, if your have one, to be signed. If you prove yourself to be sincere about the tenets of the Founders, and say you will support and defend the Constitution, I will do everything I can to help you get elected.

But if you do not agree with the values and principles of the Founding Fathers, as expressed in these books, I will do everything in my power to cause your defeat. Also, if you resort to negative personal attacks on your opponents, it will be a clear sign to me that you are not secure enough in your positions to articulate them.

We have got to return America to a true state of financial stability, political sanity, and a national character of self-reliance and personal responsibility! If you stand for these things, please speak about them at every campaign event, debate, and interview. Please let me know where you stand so I will know how to vote!

No matter which side of the political battlefield you are on, rest assured that I will be praying that God will grant you wisdom and strength to stand up for the original intent of the Constitution!

Sincerely,

A Serious Voter

ENDNOTES

Introduction

1. The Declaration of Independence
2. Proverbs 22:7
3. Article by John R. Lott, Jr., FOXNews.com, June 24, 2009
4. Official United States Oath of Office
5. John 6:44

Chapter One: Was it Just a Dream?

1. The Epic of America, by James Truslow Adams
2. Romans 1:24
3. Proverbs 20:4
4. Jeremiah 17:8
5. 2 Corinthians 13:5

Chapter Two: American Values and Founding Principles

1. Matthew 5:6
2. Leviticus 19:11
3. Exodus 20:17
4. Ezekiel 18:20
5. Deuteronomy 5:21
6. Romans 2:14
7. Official United States Oath of Office
8. Isaiah 58:2
9. Exodus 23:1
10. Second Amendment to the Constitution
11. Luke 6:31
12. Jeremiah 38:4; Proverbs 3:30
13. Luke 6:44
14. Matthew 19:21

Endnotes

Chapter Three: Says Who?

1. Proverbs Chapter 2
2. Psalm 19:1, Romans 1:20
3. Genesis 1:26-27
4. Romans 1:18-27
5. Ephesians 5:15-17
6. 1 Corinthians 1:25
7. *The Field*, by Lynne McTaggert, Harper Collins Publisher, 2002
8. John 1:9
9. 1John 1:5
10. Exodus 34:29
11. John 6:65
12. Acts 4:8-12
13. Exodus 20:3
14. John Locke, The Second Treatise of Government, paragraph 26
15. Ibid., paragraphs 123 & 124

Chapter Four: Pretty Rocks

1. From the Communist Manifesto

Chapter Five: What's Wrong with Socialism?

1. Psalm 41:1; Proverbs 28:27; 29:7;31:9. Matthew 25:35, 42; 26:11, 1 John 3:17, etc...
2. John 3:16
3. Romans 3:26
4. Romans 3:23
5. Romans 3:28 & 5:23
6. Vladimir Putin at World Economic Summit 2009, Davos, Switzerland
7. Proverbs 22:7

Chapter Six: Parallel Nations

1. IRS data from 2006 Tax Returns
2. Arthur C. Brooks, *A Nation of Givers*, American Magazine, March 2008

3. Matthew 26:11

Chapter Seven: The Five Step Plan
1. Proverbs 13:16 & 20
2. USA TODAY 5/27/2009
3. Matthew 22:21

Chapter Eight: The Fair Tax
1. Matthew 6:1-45
2. Romans 13:1
3. Proverbs 1:2-5, 2:9, 31:9, Ecc 5:8

Chapter Nine: Get Back to the Constitution

1. American Institute for Economic Research,.Economic Education Bulletin,Vol. XLV No. 12
2. Galatians 5:13
3. Psalm 96:13
4. Exodus 20:17
5. Psalm 12:5
6. Luke 12:23

Chapter Ten: Right Revolution
1. James 1:27
2. Luke 18:27
3. Matthew 19:26
4. 2 Kings 6:8-22
5. Mark 9:23; Proverbs 3 all

About the Author

Author, speaker, publisher, businessman, and philosopher, C. Jesse Duke is passionate about spreading the wealth of individual liberty, personal responsibility, and self-reliance. His previous book, **Own Yourself: A Challenge to Strong, Brave, Intelligent Young Men**, was widely and well received as precursor to this book.

Except for a period of six years in the Marine Corps, Mr. Duke has been a self-employed small business owner for thirty-eight years. He is now working as a community disorganizer to motivate Americans to once again become rugged individualists who do not rely on government, but on God, and to work to downsize government, respect the Constitution, replace the income tax with the Fair Tax, and return America to its founding principles.

About the Cover

The "Get Back!" flag on the cover of this book was designed and copyrighted by Mr. Duke as a symbol of all that Americans need to demand from government. The words "Get Back!" mean: Get back or get bit! Leave us alone, and let us go about the business of free men and women.

Although the stripes are similar in color and number to the American flag, they are not the same. The red stripes represent the blood of the patriots who have fought and died for our freedoms. The white stripes represent the holiness of God who once reigned in the hearts of most Americans, and who will reign again. The yellow corner with the rattlesnake in the grass came from the Gadsden Flag that was designed by Colonel Christopher Gadsden in 1775 to warn the British government. The original words under the snake were: "Don't Tread On Me." Altogether these symbols represent an ideal government that stays out of the way of individuals and protects and defends their freedoms.

Breinigsville, PA USA
05 March 2010
233693BV00001B/4/P